CAT

IT'S ONLY A MOVIE

WOMAN

CATW

IT'S ONLY A MOVIE

OMAN

WILL **PFEIFER** WRITER DAVID **LOPEZ** PENCILLER ALVARO **LOPEZ** INKER
JEROMY **COX** COLORIST JARED K. **FLETCHER** LETTERER
ADAM **HUGHES** ORIGINAL COVERS

CATWOMAN: IT'S ONLY A MOVIE

DC Comics, 1700 Broadway, New York, NY 10019
A Warner Bros. Entertainment Company
Printed in Canada. First Printing.
ISBN: 1-4012-1337-5
ISBN: 978-1-4012-1337-4
Cover art by Adam Hughes

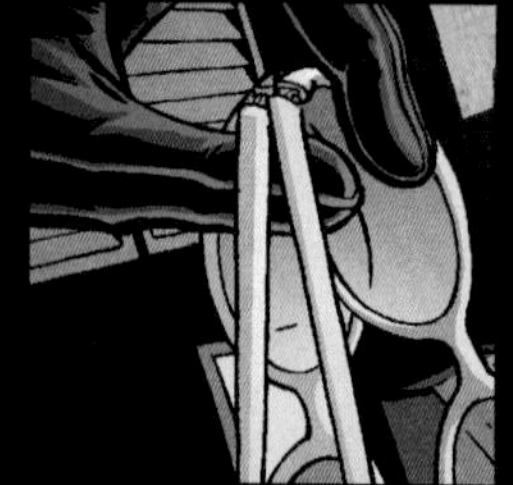

AND... *ACTION!*

MY NAME IS...
WELL, THAT'S *NOT* REALLY IMPORTANT.
YOU CAN CALL ME *EDISON,* OR YOU CAN CALL ME BY MY *CHARACTER'S* NAME...
CALL ME THE *FILM FREAK.*

UNTIL YESTERDAY, I CO-STARRED WITH A MAN NAMED BEND. *ANGLE MAN.*
I STUCK WITH HIM BECAUSE I THOUGHT THIS WAS *HIS* MOVIE.

I THOUGHT I WAS JUST A *SUPPORTING* CHARACTER. "VILLAIN NO. 2." THAT SORT OF THING.

THEN I *CHANGED* MY MIND.
AS SOON AS WE WENT UP AGAINST *CATWOMAN,* I REALIZED THE MOVIE WAS ABOUT *HER.*
SEXY, ACTION-PACKED.
A SUMMER *BLOCK-BUSTER.*

BUT I WAS WRONG *AGAIN.*
IT'S NOT A MOVIE ABOUT CATWOMAN-- OR ANGLE MAN-- NO MATTER *HOW* GOOD THEIR NAMES MIGHT LOOK UP ON A MARQUEE.

IT'S A MOVIE ABOUT *ME.*
I'M THE MAIN CHARACTER.
THAT MEANS WHEN THE END CREDITS *FINALLY* ROLL...
I'LL BE THE *ONLY* ONE LEFT STANDING.

IS THAT IT?
NO. ONE MORE THING. A BIT OF AN HOMAGE TO A FILM CLASSIC.
WHAT? WHICH ONE?
"THE GREAT TRAIN ROBBERY."
BLAM
AND... CUT.
♪
HOORAY FOR HOLLYWOOD... ♪

GET OFFA ME, SELINA!
THE NAME IS IRENA, SMART BOMB...
"SMART BOMB"? BUT I'M...

HEY! BRADLEY!
WHO...?

SAY YOUR PRAYERS!

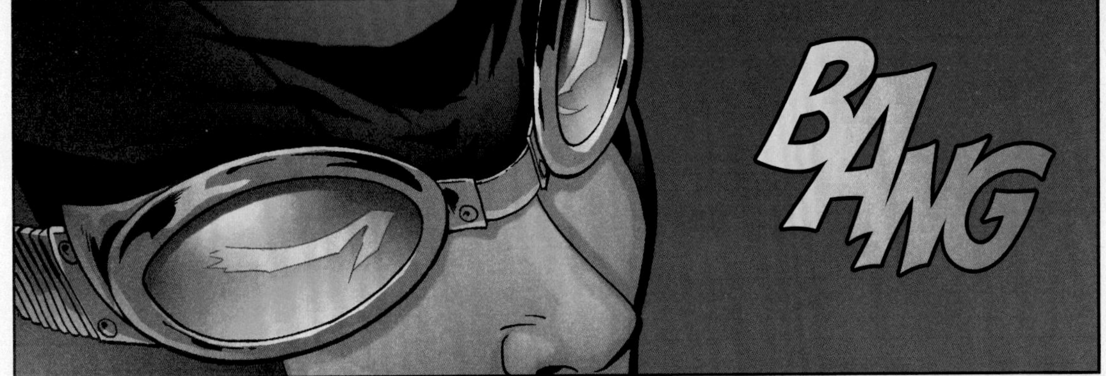
BANG

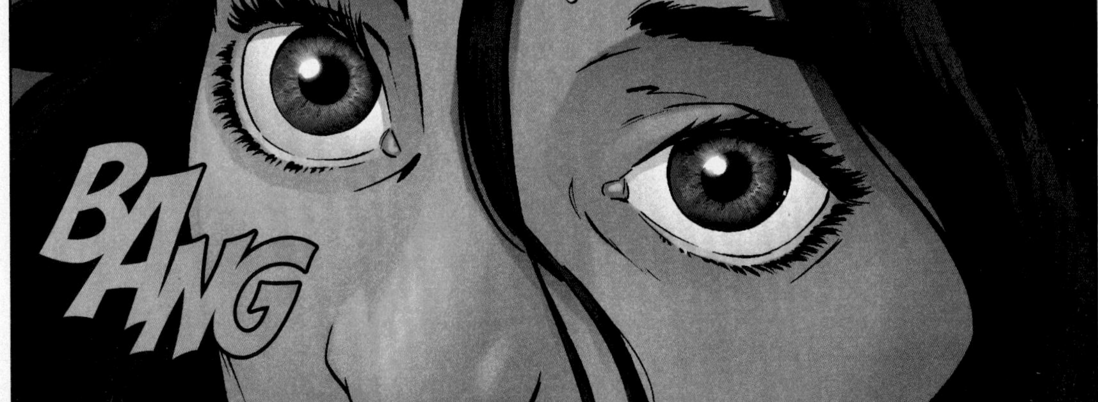
BANG

BANG
BANG
BANG
BANG
SAM?
WUH... WUH... WUH...
GOTHAM
AL

SELINA! OPEN UP!
I NEED TO TALK TO YOU!
BANG BANG

SELINA?
TED. HI.
HELENA, PLEASE. MOMMY AND MR. GRANT HAVE TO TALK. PLEASE.
WAAAAAAH!

CUTE KID.
YES, SHE IS.
WHAT BRINGS YOU AROUND? I THOUGHT YOU AND HOLLY WERE BUSY KEEPING THE EAST END SAFE FOR DECENT PEOPLE.
WAAAAAAH!

WE WERE. THEN HOLLY GOT ARRESTED.
SHE'S IN JAIL RIGHT NOW.

WHAT?

WELL THEN, WHAT ARE WE DOING HERE? LET'S GET HER OUT!
I DON'T KNOW HOW MUCH HER BAIL IS, BUT BELIEVE ME, I HAVE MORE THAN ENOUGH--

IT'S NOT EXACTLY A BAIL-ABLE OFFENSE, SELINA.
IT'S MURDER.

MURDER? HOLLY?
THE COPS-- ONE IN PARTICULAR, FROM WHAT I COULD TELL-- THINK SHE KILLED WHAT'S HIS NAME... THAT EAST END BASTARD, DIED ABOUT A YEAR AGO...
BLACK MASK?
YEAH. HIM. THEY THINK SHE KILLED HIM. OR AT LEAST, THEY THINK CATWOMAN KILLED HIM.
MY GOD.

BUT... IF SHE'S IN JAIL... IF SHE'S FACING MURDER CHARGES...
WELL, NO OFFENSE, TED, BUT WHY DID SHE CALL YOU? WHY DIDN'T SHE CALL ME?

OH. RIGHT.
YEP. YOU'VE GOT A WHOLE NEW SET OF RESPONSIBILITIES NOW.

YOU'RE RIGHT. I DO.

BUT I STILL HAVE THE OLD ONES, TOO.
WE HAVE TO DO SOMETHING FOR HOLLY, TED. WE HAVE TO GET HER OUT OF THERE.

HELLO?
DETECTIVE LENAHAN?
HOW LONG ARE YOU GOING TO LET HER SIT AND STEW, LENAHAN? THAT COSTUME'S GOT TO BE GETTING A BIT RIPE.
ANYBODY?
HEY, I DIDN'T FORCE HER TO WEAR THAT GETUP. AND I'M JUST KEEPING HER UNTIL ONE OF TWO THINGS HAPPENS. EITHER SHE CONFESSES...
OR THE REAL CATWOMAN-- THE ONE WHO REALLY KILLED BLACK MASK-- SHOWS UP. EITHER WAY, I FIGURE MY JOB IS DONE.
BESIDES, SHE GOT HER ONE PHONE CALL. HELL, I EVEN LET HER SLEEP IN A NICE, COZY HOLDING CELL LAST NIGHT.
KOBAYASHI
I'M SURE THAT WENT WELL.
YOU CAN'T HOLD HER FOREVER, YOU KNOW. IT'S NOT LIKE IT USED TO BE.
THE WAR ON COSTUMES IS OVER. GORDON IS BACK IN CHARGE.
GORDON?
THAT'S GOTHAM PROPER, THIS IS THE EAST END.
THERE'S A BIG DIFFERENCE.

GIMME A SEC. I GOTTA GET A CUP OF COFFEE. GIVING THAT GIRL THE THIRD DEGREE IS STARTING TO--
HEY! WHAT THE HELL'S GOING ON?
WHAT? DIDN'T YOU HEAR?
POLICE
NO. I DIDN'T. SUPPOSE YOU TELL ME.
IT WAS THOSE TWO ROOKIES-- BRENT AND KEENAN? THE ONES WHO JUST GOT HERE A WEEK AGO?
THEY WERE TRYING TO STOP A ROBBERY AND... WELL, THEY GOT KILLED.
BOTH OF THEM? WHAT WAS IT? BANK ROBBERY? ARMORED CAR?
NOPE. A CONVENIENCE STORE.
WHAT? NO WAY. HOW MANY GUYS?
JUST ONE. AND ALL HE STOLE WAS A PACK OF GUM.
GUM? THEN HOW DID HE KILL THEM? GUN? KNIFE?
"NOPE.
"BUILDING."
CHINESE FOOD
take away
Today only
Spain
vs.

C'MON, BUDDY. IT'S A PACK OF **GUM.** YOU DON'T WANT TO GO TO **JAIL** FOR THIS.

HAND IT OVER. I'M SURE WE CAN TALK THE OWNER INTO **NOT** PRESSING CHARGES.

JUST GIVE US THE DAMN **GUM,** OK?

"SO HE **DOES.**
"I MEAN, HE **DROPS** IT.

"IT'S ONLY **GUM,** RIGHT? BUT THERE'S **SOMETHING** ABOUT THIS GUY. SOMETHING SEEMS A LITTLE **HINKY.**
"SO BRENT AND KEENAN, THEY PLAY IT **SAFE.** THEY TELL HIM TO PUT HIS **HANDS** UP."
GOOD... GOOD...
NOW, IF YOU COULD JUST PUT YOUR HANDS UP...

"SO HE **DOES.**

"AND THEN...
"HE DOES SOMETHING **ELSE.**"

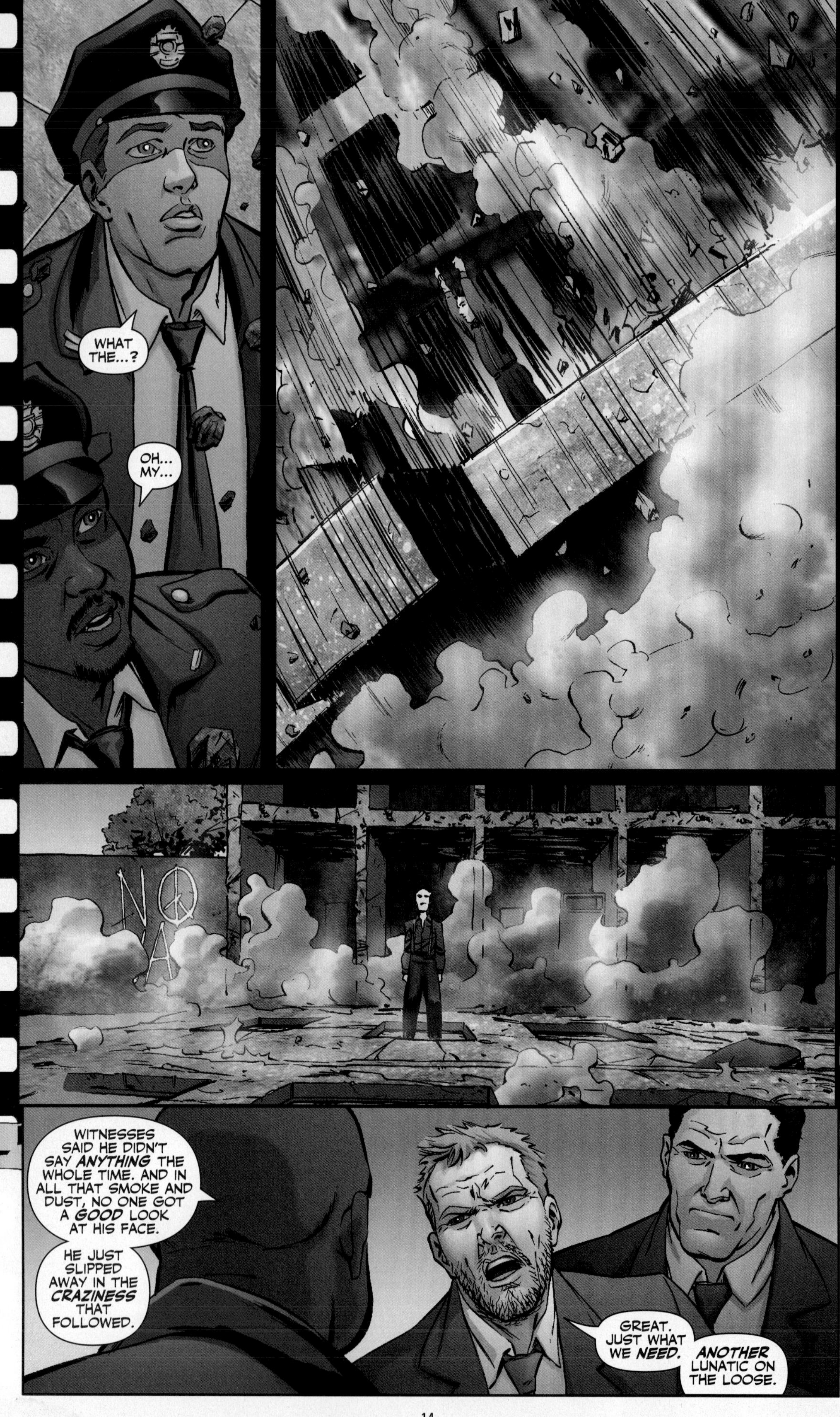

WHAT THE...?
OH... MY...
WITNESSES SAID HE DIDN'T SAY ANYTHING THE WHOLE TIME. AND IN ALL THAT SMOKE AND DUST, NO ONE GOT A GOOD LOOK AT HIS FACE.
HE JUST SLIPPED AWAY IN THE CRAZINESS THAT FOLLOWED.
GREAT. JUST WHAT WE NEED. ANOTHER LUNATIC ON THE LOOSE.

OKAY. LET ME THINK THIS THROUGH.
GETTING IN SHOULDN'T BE MUCH OF A PROBLEM. IT'S GETTING OUT-- AND STAYING OUT-- THAT'S GOING TO BE TRICKY.
AND THAT'S WHERE YOU COME IN. YOU AND YOUR FRIENDS.
MY FRIENDS?
SURE. THE JUSTICE SOCIETY.
OBVIOUSLY GREEN LANTERN WILL BE ESSENTIAL FOR SOMETHING LIKE THIS, BUT THE OTHERS CAN ALSO--
WHOA, WHOA, WHOA. THAT'S JUST WHAT HOLLY SAID, AND IT'S NOT GOING TO HAPPEN. THAT'S NOT THE WAY WE DO THINGS.
WE DON'T BREAK PEOPLE OUT OF JAIL. WE DON'T BREAK THE LAW.
YOU'RE KIDDING, RIGHT?
I DON'T GET YOU PEOPLE. YOU CALL YOURSELVES THE "JUSTICE" SOCIETY, BUT YOU CARE MORE ABOUT THE LAW THAN JUSTICE.
YOU KNOW SHE'S INNOCENT, AND YOU KNOW THE ONLY WAY SHE'S GETTING OUT IS IF WE GET HER OUT, BUT YOU STILL WON'T DO ANYTHING ABOUT IT?
I DON'T SEE WHY THE HELL YOU DON'T JUST TRADE IN YOUR COSTUMES FOR SOME POLICE UNIFORMS. SEEMS THEY'D FIT JUST AS WELL!
SLAM
SELINA?

CAN I AT LEAST ASK YOU FOR ONE SMALL FAVOR?
I PROMISE IT WON'T INVOLVE YOU BREAKING ANY OF THE SOCIETY'S PRECIOUS RULES.
SURE, SELINA. I MEAN, I--
GOOD.
WATCH HELENA.
IF SHE CRIES, FEED HER. OR COMFORT HER. OR CHANGE HER. IT'S THAT SIMPLE.
O...OKAY...
I WON'T BE GONE LONG.
I HAVE TO SEE A MAN ABOUT A COP.

WAIT A MINUTE...
THIS ISN'T EVEN LOCKED.
SORRY I DIDN'T JUST COME IN THE FRONT DOOR, BUT SEEING AS HOW I'M WANTED FOR MURDER ONE, I DIDN'T THINK...
SLAM?
SLAM?
HELLO?
KLIK
SLAM? THIS IS KARON. HAVE YOU SEEN HOLLY?
BEEP
SLAM? IT'S KARON AGAIN. PLEASE--
BEEP
SLAM? IT'S KARON. I REALLY--
BEEP
PLEASE, SLAM. IT'S KARON. I'M GETTING--

KARON. YOU POOR KID...
YOU MUST BE WORRIED SICK--
EH?
GOTHAM

SLAM?
I...

OH, SLAM.

SLAM? SLAM, ARE YOU OKAY?
SELINA? JEEZ, KID. WHAT BRINGS YOU HERE? COME TO CHECK UP ON POOR OL' SLAM?
POOR, PATHETIC SLAM CAN'T HOLD HIS BOOZE. IS THAT IT?

NO. IT'S HOLLY. SHE'S IN TROUBLE. BIG TROUBLE. WITH THE POLICE.

I NEED HELP, SLAM...
DO YOU HAVE ANY FRIENDS LEFT ON THE FORCE?

NE YEAR AGO, VE OR TAKE...
THE EAST END...
SO WHAT ARE WE TALKING ABOUT HERE, SELINA? HE'S DEAD, RIGHT?
BLACK MASK? OH, YEAH. I'M SURE OF IT.
BUT JUST BECAUSE THE HEAD'S BEEN CU OFF, THAT DOESN MEAN THE BODY IS STILL TWITCHING TWITCHING VIOLENTLY.
HE HAD FRIENDS-- FLUNKIES, ACTUALLY-- AND THEY'LL KEEP AT IT UNTIL WE'RE DEAD-- OR THEY ARE.
THAT SKULL-HEADED BASTARD INSPIRED SOME FIERCE LOYALTY, I'LL GIVE HIM THAT.
YOU'RE TELLING ME.
UTE LEMPER
WHAT HE DID TO ME... TO YOU. WHAT HE DID TO MY DAD.
IT CAN'T GO ON. I MEAN, SOMEONE'S GOT TO PUT AN END TO IT, ONCE AND FOR ALL.
BUT YOU'RE A COP, SAM.
HA. NOT ANYMORE. THESE DAYS, I'M EVEN LESS LEGAL THAN YOU.
I WANT TO DO THIS, SELINA. FOR MY DAD.
AND FOR YOU.
THEN I THINK THERE'S ONE OTHER THING WE NEED TO TALK ABOUT.

THIS MIGHT SOUND OFF-THE-WALL, SAM. HELL, IT FEELS STRANGE JUST SAYING IT. BUT THERE'S SOMETHING BETWEEN US, AND IT ISN'T JUST BLACK MASK.
EVER SINCE WE WERE BOTH FAKE BADGUYS FOR HUGO STRANGE, ME IN MY CATSUIT AND YOU IN YOUR ROCKET ARMOR, THERE'S BEEN... A CONNECTION.
UTE LEMPER
I CAN'T EXPLAIN IT, BUT THERE IT IS. I FIGURED AS LONG AS WE'RE MAKING A BLOOD PACT, WE MIGHT AS WELL BRING OUR FEELINGS OUT IN THE OPEN.
SO TELL ME-- AM I CRAZY? AM I READING THIS WRONG? HAVE ALL THOSE YEARS OF STARING THROUGH GOGGLES WARPED MY VISION?
NO. THEY HAVEN'T. YOU'RE NOT. BUT ISN'T THIS-- YOU KNOW, GIVEN THE TIMING, AND WELL, GIVEN HOW WE MET-- ISN'T IT JUST A LITTLE TOO WEIRD?
WEIRD?
YOU WERE A COP IN A JETPACK PRETENDING TO BE A SUPER-VILLAIN.
IN MY WORLD, THAT'S WARD CLEAVER NORMAL.
BUT...
SAM. WE'RE ATTRACTED TO EACH OTHER. WE'RE GETTING READY TO "TEAM UP."
AND IN A COUPLE OF DAYS, WE COULD BOTH BE DEAD. I THINK IT'S TIME FOR US TO ACT LIKE ADULTS.
YOU'RE RIGHT, SELINA, YOU'RE RIGHT. IT'S JUST THAT I...
GOOD.
NOW SHUT UP AND KISS ME.

THERE'S **NO** ONE? NO ONE ELSE, I MEAN? I'M ***DESPERATE,*** SLAM. I NEED TO GET HOLLY OUT OF THERE. AND ***SOON.***

NO... THERE'S NO ONE...

NO ONE BUT **SAM.**

AND FINALLY, A SAD, **STRANGE** STORY FROM GOTHAM'S EAST END, WHERE A CLASSIC MOVIE SCENE WAS REPLAYED-- WITH **HORRIFYING** RESULTS.

ARLENE OWENS, 29, WAS EATING LUNCH AT A SIDE-WALK CAFE WHEN AN **UNIDENTIFIED** MAN WALKED UP TO HER TABLE AND PUSHED A **GRAPEFRUIT** INTO HER FACE...

ONE WITNESS LIKENED IT TO A SCENE FROM THE 1931 JIMMY CAGNEY CLASSIC, **"THE PUBLIC ENEMY."**

ONLY **THIS** TIME, THE GRAPEFRUIT WAS SOAKED IN **ACID.** OWENS WAS RUSHED TO GOTHAM MEMORIAL, WHERE HER CONDITION IS LISTED AS **CRITICAL.**

DOCTORS **REFUSED** TO DISCUSS THE DAMAGE TO HER FACE.

THE ASSAILANT, WHO SLIPPED AWAY IN THE CROWD, REMAINS AT LARGE.
SEE, KID?

IT'S A TERRIBLE WORLD OUT THERE.
AND IT'S WAY PAST SAVING.

S.T.A.R. LABS? WHAT? YOU WORK THERE?
SORT OF. TONIGHT'S MY FIRST NIGHT. GRAVEYARD SHIFT. MAINTENANCE.
WHAT WAS IT? YEAR, YEAR AND A HALF AGO, SOME MONSTER BROKE OUT OF THERE, WRECKED THE PLACE.
BUDDY OF MINE WORKED THERE, SAID THEIR BUDGET GOT SLASHED. SECURITY, STAFFING, YOU NAME IT.
THAT'S WHAT THEY SAY.
ZUTATEN

YOU DRIVE A CAB. HAVE YOU EVER SEEN THE MOVIE "TAXI!"?
WHAT? "TAXI DRIVER"? WITH BOBBY D? SURE! LOTSA TIMES! THAT ENDING, MAN, IT'S IN-TENSE!
TAXI
TX4472

NO. NOT "TAXI DRIVER." JUST "TAXI!"
WHAT? LIKE THE TV SHOW? THE ONE WITH THAT GUY FROM THE OTHER SHOW? YEAH, I SAW IT A COUPLE OF TIMES ON NICK AT NITE. PRETTY FUNNY, I GUESS.

NO. NOT THE TV SHOW. THE MOVIE. THE ONE THAT STARRED JIMMY--
FALLON, RIGHT? YEAH! IT STARRED JIMMY FALLON! MAN, THAT WAS HILARIOUS!

QUEEN LATIFAH WAS IN IT, AND IT HAD THOSE HOT CHICKS ROBBING BANKS AND STUFF? AND THAT CAR WAS TRICKED OUT! THAT MOVIE WAS GREAT!
NO. NOT FALLON. CAGNEY. JIMMY CAGNEY.
WHO?

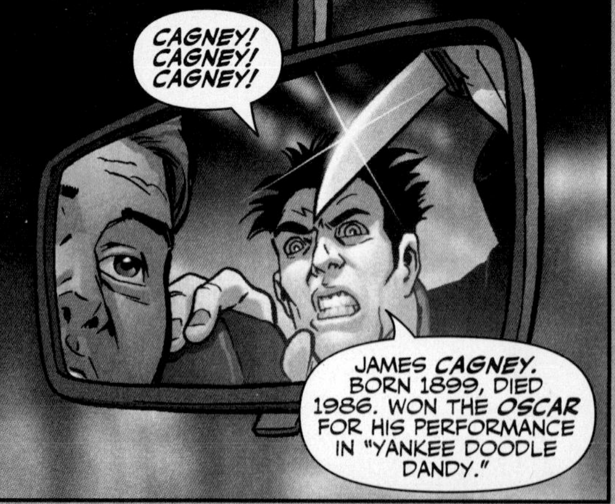
CAGNEY! CAGNEY! CAGNEY!
JAMES CAGNEY. BORN 1899, DIED 1986. WON THE OSCAR FOR HIS PERFORMANCE IN "YANKEE DOODLE DANDY."

ALSO APPEARED IN "ONE, TWO, THREE," "THE ROARING TWENTIES," "ANGELS WITH DIRTY FACES," AND "RAGTIME"...
AAAUGH! GOD! NO! PLEASE!
STAB STAB STAB STAB STAB
THOUGH HE'S PERHAPS BEST REMEMBERED FOR HIS PERFORMANCE IN THE 1931 FILM "THE PUBLIC ENEMY," WHERE, IN AN ICONIC SCENE--

--HE SMASHES A GRAPEFRUIT IN MAE CLARKE'S FACE.

KERRASH

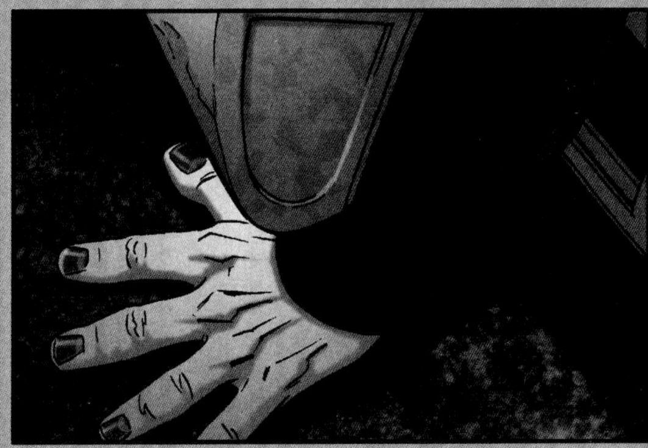

CAGNEY. JIMMY CAGNEY.
NEXT TIME, GET IT RIGHT. OKAY?

NOW. WHERE AM--

S.T.A.R.
Scientific and Technological Advanced Research Laboratories
AH. PERFECT.
A FLAWLESS CHANGE OF LOCATION.

BRIIING BRIIING
JUST A SECOND, JUST A SECOND...
C'MON, HELENA. YOU GOTTA HOLD STILL, KIDDO...
PLEASE?

HELLO?
TED? IT'S SELINA. HOW'S EVERYTHING GOING? HOW'S MY GIRL?
FINE. SHE'S FINE. EVERYTHING'S FINE. WE'RE HAVING A HELL-- A HECKUVA TIME HERE. SHE REALLY LIKES THE MASK, BY THE WAY. I MEAN REALLY LIKES IT.
SO, YOU COMING BACK SOON?

NOT EXACTLY...
GOTHAM CITY
DEPARTMENT OF REC

I'M WORKING ON SOMETHING RIGHT NOW. I'D REALLY APPRECIATE IT IF YOU COULD WATCH HER FOR ANOTHER HOUR, TED.
JUST ONE MORE. I'D OWE YOU BIG TIME.
WHAT? OKAY, SURE. BUT WHAT ARE YOU DOING?

I WISH I COULD TELL YOU, TED. I REALLY DO.

Gotham City
Police Department
East End Precinct
BUT IT'S COMPLICATED.

I REALIZE THAT, AS I NEAR *THE* END OF THE FIRST ACT, MY MOVIE IS ABOUT TO MAKE A CONTROVERSIAL *TWIST.*
THE CRITICS ARE *NOT* GOING TO LIKE THIS.

Owens, Arlene
Processing
TO *HELL* WITH THEM. FILM CRITICISM IS A *DEAD* ART ANYWAY. IT'S ALL THUMBS AND STARS AND LETTER GRADES.

FILM DOESN'T REQUIRE *BLAND* APPRAISALS. IT REQUIRES *BOLD* CHOICES.
THIS MOVIE CAN'T BE *PREDICTABLE,* OR SAFE, OR *AFRAID* TO TAKE CHANCES.
Arlene Owens

I MUST *UP* THE ANTE. *RAISE* THE STAKES.
ACT ONE INCLUDED SILENT *SLAPSTICK* AND GANGSTER *VIOLENCE.* THAT WON'T BE ENOUGH FOR ACT *TWO.*

MOVIE AUDIENCES GROW *JADED* QUICKLY.
I HAVE TO SHOW THEM SOME-THING *NEW.* SOMETHING *AMAZING.*
HEY! HOLD IT RIGHT--

BLAM

AS I WAS SAYING, YOU HAVE TO STUN AN AUDIENCE.
SHOCK THEM. SHOW THEM SOME-THING THAT WILL MAKE THEM GASP.
SOMETHING THEY MIGHT *HATE* AT FIRST. MIGHT FEAR. MIGHT NOT EVEN *BELIEVE.*
BUT I'M READY. I'VE REACHED THE *RIGHT* MOMENT.
IT'S *TIME.*

"STEAMBOAT BILL JR." 1928. "THE PUBLIC ENEMY." *1931.* "TAXI!" *1932.* THAT BRINGS US TO *1933.*
QUITE A YEAR FOR CINEMA.
ENTRY.
LIVE SPECIMEN

IT WAS THE YEAR OF "THE *INVISIBLE* MAN" AND "THE TESTAMENT OF DR. *MABUSE.*" OF "THE MYSTERY OF THE *WAX* MUSEUM" AND "THE VAMPIRE *BAT.*"
BUT THAT'S *NOT* ALL.

1933 WAS *ALSO* THE YEAR THAT HOLLYWOOD LEARNED, ONCE AND FOR *ALL*...
THAT FOR SHEER *DRAMA,* FOR SHEER *SPECTACLE*...

Technological Advanced Rese
S.T.A.R.
...NOTHING TOPS...
A GIANT GORILLA.

NO
TRESPASSING

S.T.A.R.

EXPLOSIVE

ROSEBUD.

SKABOOM
WHAT THE HELL WAS THAT?
I--
RRRRR...

THOSE LAB BOYS REALLY DID A NUMBER ON YOU, DIDN'T THEY? TOOK A MAGNIFICENT BEAST LIKE YOURSELF AND STUCK HIM IN HIGH-TECH, REMOTE-CONTROLLED CHAINS.
WELL, I'M GOING TO SHUT IT OFF, THROW IT AWAY AND LET YOU HAVE YOUR FUN. BUT FORGIVE ME IF I DON'T STICK AROUND TO WATCH. AFTER ALL --
I KNOW HOW YOUR MOVIE ENDS.

PLEASE. PLEASE.
I'M CATWOMAN. I'M HER. I REALLY AM.
WHY WON'T YOU BELIEVE ME?

YOU'RE JOKING, RIGHT?

THE REAL CATWOMAN WOULDN'T BE HERE, WHIMPERING LIKE A SCARED LITTLE KID.
HELL, THE REAL CATWOMAN WOULDN'T HAVE BEEN ARRESTED SO EASILY IN THE FIRST PLACE.
A DOZEN COPS? FIFTY? A HUNDRED? WOULDN'T HAVE MATTERED. NOT TO HER.

NO, YOU'RE NOT HER. BUT YOU DO KNOW HER, DON'T YOU? YOU KNOW HER WELL.
YEAH, YOU DO.
C'MON, KID. JUST GIVE ME A NAME. HELL, JUST GIVE ME A LAST NAME.
ONE WORD TO THE WISE AND YOU GET OUT OF JAIL FREE. NO STRINGS ATTACHED.

SHE'S A HERO, RIGHT? BRAVE, TOUGH, SELF-SACRIFICING?
TRUST ME, KID. I KNOW HER TYPE. SHE'D UNDERSTAND. SHE'D HATE TO SEE YOU SUFFER LIKE THIS.
I...

LENAHAN!

Air vents. Ha. As if they would actually hold anyone.
Movies. Can't count on them for any real information.
Luckily, you can count on the sort of low-level municipal graft that results in a 12-inch crawlspace getting installed by the councilman's contractor brother-in-law.
Thanks, graft!
Which, if those blueprints were right, should put me right above the detective's interrogation room.
TAP TAP TAP
PLINK
WHU--?
BINGO.

This plaster is typical low-grade, low-bid municipal issue. One good whack should get me through.
Now all I need is some sort of distraction.

Typical cops. Always talk so loud you can hear them three rooms away.
Thanks, cops.
THIS HAD BETTER BE GOOD.

I'M ABOUT SIX SECONDS FROM SEEING THREE DAYS OF DAMN NEAR NONSTOP INTERROGATION FINALLY PAY OFF.
SORRY, JIMBO. GONNA HAVE TO COME BACK TO IT.

BIG EMERGENCY. BIG. BIG. SWAT TEAM'S ALREADY BEEN SCRAMBLED. REINFORCEMENTS ARE COMING FROM DOWN-TOWN.
AND CAP WANTS EVERY SHIELD AND UNIFORM ON THE STREET. NOW.
WHY? WHAT'S SO DAMNED URGENT?
APE. BIG APE.
BIG BIG BIG APE.
GREAT. CAMPBELL, YOU STAY RIGHT HERE.
MAKE SURE MY GUEST DOESN'T LEAVE THE PARTY BEFORE I GET BACK.
YES SIR!

A BIG APE?
THAT'LL DO.
THANKS, BIG APE.

KERRASH
YAAAAH!
SHHH
SSSSSS
WHAT THE HELL IS GO--
WOK
UNGH!

I HAVE TO SAY, THAT WAS MUCH EASIER THAN I THOUGHT IT WOULD BE.
OF COURSE, GETTING OUT IS GOING TO BE THE REAL TRICK. EVEN WITH A GIANT APE, I--
OH MY GOD...
SE--
CATWOMAN.
YOU REALLY DID IT. YOU REALLY CAME FOR ME.
YOU BET I DID, KID.
NOW C'MON. LET'S GET YOU HOME.

OKAY. WE'RE OUT OF THE STATION, BUT WE'RE NOT OUT OF THE WOODS.
NOT YET.
STICK WITH ME, HOLLY, AND STAY IN THE SHADOWS.
COUPLE OF WOMEN ON THE ROOF OF POLICE HEADQUARTERS IN LEATHER CATSUITS?
THAT'S BOUND TO ATTRACT ATTENTION.
G.C.P.D.
POLICE
BLAM
BLAM
GAAAHHH!
POLICE
BLAM
BLAM
BLAM
OR MAYBE NOT.
POLICE

JEEZ, SELINA! WHAT THE HELL IS IT?
BLAM
GAAAHHH!
GRRRRRR!
BLAM BLAM
IT'S A GIANT GORILLA, HOLLY. WHAT DOES IT LOOK LIKE?
"WELL, DUH. I CAN SEE THAT. I MEAN WHERE DID IT COME FROM?"
G.C.P.D.
THESE RIFLES ARE USELESS! WE'RE NEVER GONNA STOP HIM!
THEY'RE BRINGING IN THE ROCKET LAUNCHER. SHOULD BE HERE ANY SECOND. THAT'LL STOP HIM.
"WE LIVE IN A STRANGE WORLD, HOLLY. THERE ARE A LOT OF GIANT GORILLAS OUT THERE.
"WHOLE BUNCH OF 'EM ATTACKED NEW YORK COUPLE OF YEARS AGO. MAYBE THIS IS ONE OF THEM."
REALLY? WELL, THERE'S GONNA BE ONE LESS IN A MINUTE OR SO.
GOTHAM'S FINEST ARE GONNA SEE TO THAT.
"SELINA?"
OKAY! GET THAT THING INTO POSITION!
SWAT
WE HAVE TO DO SOMETHING, HOLLY.
WE HAVE TO SAVE THAT POOR, DUMB APE.

WHAT?!? ARE YOU JOKING?!?
SELINA, LET THE COPS HANDLE THIS ONE! IT'S WHAT THEY'RE GOOD FOR! IT'S ALL THEY'RE GOOD FOR!
THEY'RE GOING TO SLAUGHTER HIM, HOLLY. THOSE SWAT BOYS CAN'T WAIT FOR THE KILL ORDER.
SO?
SO THIS IS WHAT WE DO, HOLLY. THIS IS WHAT CATWOMAN DOES.
SHE PROTECTS THE INNOCENT.
HOLLY, YOU'VE BEEN THROUGH A LOT. AND YOU'VE BEEN SO BRAVE. I CAN HANDLE THIS ONE.
THE GIANT KILLER APE. YOU CAN HANDLE HIM ALL BY YOURSELF. NOT TO MENTION ALL THOSE COPS, WHO HAPPEN TO BE LOOKING FOR YOU.
SURE. NO PROBLEM.
AND WHAT IF YOU GET KILLED?
THEN I GET KILLED.
GO HOME, HOLLY. BACK TO MY APARTMENT. I'LL BE THERE SOON. AND CALL KARON. LET HER KNOW YOU'RE OKAY.
JIRO
BRIIING BRIIING
HMM?
HELLO?
HEY, TED. NO, IT'S HOLLY. YEP. SHE GOT ME OUT. JUST A FEW MINUTES AGO.
WHERE IS SHE NOW?
GUESS.

You know, in retrospect...
GAAAHHH!
YOU STILL WANT US TO FIRE, SIR? WE MIGHT HIT CATWOMAN!
JUST DON'T HIT ANY BUILDINGS. ON MY MARK...
...maybe I should have thought this one through.
TARGET ACQUIRED
FIRE!

SSSSSHHHBOOOOM
MOVE IT, YA BIG APE!
GAAAHHH!
GRRRRR!
This isn't good. I only have a few seconds before Son of Kong here bashes my brains out on the sidewalk.
Need to find something... anything...
Bingo!
YOINK!
SWAT
SIR! SHE GRABBED ONE OF MY NON-LETHALS!
LOAD THE LAUNCHER AGAIN. IF THAT MONKEY DOESN'T TAKE HER OUT...
...WE WILL.
It's nice to have your hard work appreciated.

OKAY, LANCELOT LINK. JUST THINK OF THIS AS A BIG, FAT SLEEPING PILL--
POOM
GRRRRR!
AND THIS, MY FINE, FURRY FRIEND, IS WHERE I MUST BID YOU ADIEU.
UHHH...
NEXT TIME, STAY OFF THE STREETS AFTER DARK, OKAY?
UH-OH.

POLICE
GOLDENE ZITRONE
WHOOM
ARE WE OKAY? NO ONE GOT SQUASHED FLAT BY THE GIANT APE, DID THEY?
NAW, CAP. WE'RE ALL STILL IN ONE PIECE AND THREE DIMENSIONS.
DISPATCH SAYS SOME S.T.A.R. LABS HONCHOS ARE HEADED DOWN HERE WITH A VAN. A BIG ONE.
THEN THAT ONLY LEAVES ONE QUESTION.
SWAT
"WHERE THE HELL IS THE BEAUTY THAT PUT THIS BEAST TO SLEEP?"

CUT ME OFF? THROW ME OUT? I'VE BEEN COMING TO THIS TOILET SINCE BEFORE YOUR OLD MAN WAS EVEN...
JUST GO HOME, BRADLEY! GO HOME!

FINE! FINE! I'LL TAKE MY BUSINESS ELSE-WHERE! THERE'S A LOT OF BARS IN THIS TOWN THAT'D BE PROUD TO HOST SLAM BRADLEY!
A LOT OF BARS...

GAAAH!

GREAT. JUST GREAT. TOP OF EVERY-THING ELSE, NOW I GOTTA DEAL WITH A GIANT...
AW HELL.

NOT THIS.
NOT AGAIN.

CAN'T BELIEVE IT STILL HURTS.
AFTER ALL THIS TIME.

ONE YEAR AGO...
GIVE OR TAKE...
MARTHA WAYNE MEMORIAL HOSPITAL
TOMORROW'S THE DAY, SAM. I'LL BE JOINING YOU ON THE OUTSIDE. DOC'S FINALLY GIVING ME MY WALKING PAPERS.
THEY DIDN'T WANT TO TAKE ANY CHANCES, DAD. BLACK MASK LEFT YOU IN PRETTY BAD SHAPE.

YEAH. A MESSAGE CARVED INTO MY *CHEST.* THAT FREAK LEFT ME WITH ONE *HELLUVA* SOUVENIR!
STILL, I GUESS HIS *KNIFE*-WIELDING DAYS ARE OVER, EH, SAM? HEH.
NOT THAT HE DIDN'T *DESERVE* IT, BUT WHAT'S THE SCOOP ON HIS *MURDER?* ANY SUSPECTS?
WHAT ARE YOUR *FRIENDS* ON THE FORCE SAYING?
EX-FRIENDS, DAD. *EX*-FORCE, REMEMBER? ANYHOW, MOST OF THEM BARELY CARE. GOOD *RIDDANCE,* AS FAR AS THEY'RE CONCERNED.
ONLY *ONE* GUY'S REALLY PURSUING THE CASE. HE HAS SOME CRAZY THEORY IT MIGHT'VE BEEN *CATWOMAN.*
CATWOMAN? *HA!* THAT GUY IS WAY OFF. MURDER AIN'T HER STYLE. TRUST ME ON THIS ONE. *YOU* DON'T KNOW HER LIKE *I* DO.
ACTUALLY, DAD, *THAT'S* WHAT I WANTED TO TALK TO YOU ABOUT.
MY KID. MY *OWN* KID.
PATHETIC OLD MAN.
PLEASE! *DON'T* INSULT YOURSELF!

WHAT THE...?
YOU'RE REALLY QUITE AMAZING. ESPECIALLY TO A FILM BUFF LIKE MYSELF.
YOU'RE A PERFECT MASH-UP OF TWO CLASSIC FORTIES MOVIE CLICHÉS. IT'S SO RARE TO SEE BOTH IN A SINGLE CHARACTER.
NOW THAT'S BOLD SCREENWRITING. IT SKIRTS THE EDGE OF PARODY AND PATHOS.
ON THE ONE HAND, WE'VE GOT THE ARCHETYPICAL COMEDIC DRUNK. SLOVENLY, UNSHAVEN, BARELY ABLE TO STAND.
I MEAN, LOOK AT YOU. I HALF EXPECTED YOU TO SHAKE YOUR HEAD IN DISBELIEF AND LOUDLY SWEAR OFF DRINKING WHEN YOU SAW THAT APE.
BUT THAT WOULD CONFLICT WITH CLICHÉ NUMBER TWO: THE WORLD-WEARY FILM NOIR DETECTIVE WHO FINDS SOLACE AT THE BOTTOM OF A BOTTLE.
ON ITS OWN, A CLASSIC ARCHETYPE. BUT COMBINED WITH THE OTHER...?
SHEER BRILLIANCE.
STILL, I MUST ADMIT, YOUR CHARACTER ARC SEEMS DANGEROUSLY STEEP.
BAR
IF I WERE YOU, I'D START PRAYING FOR A THIRD ACT MIRACLE.

IT'S *OKAY,* HELENA... MAMA'S HOME. MAMA'S HOME.

WHAT'S THE MATTER, KIDDO? WHY ARE YOU SO *FUSSY* ALL OF A...

OH, MY GOD...

I THINK TED PUT THIS DIAPER ON *BACKWARDS.* AH, WELL. IT WAS A LONG NIGHT FOR *ALL* OF US.

CRAZY ONE, TOO, BY THE LOOKS OF THINGS-- ESPECIALLY IN THE EAST END.

TWO COPS GET KILLED BY A FALLING *BUILDING.* SOME WOMAN GETS HIT IN THE FACE WITH A *GRAPEFRUIT* FULL OF ACID.

AND, OF COURSE, THE *GIANT APE.* BUT YOU *KNEW* ABOUT THAT ONE.

WAIT A MINUTE.
HOUSE FALLS ON *COPS.* IT'S FROM A KEATON MOVIE. "STEAMBOAT BILL, JR." 1928.

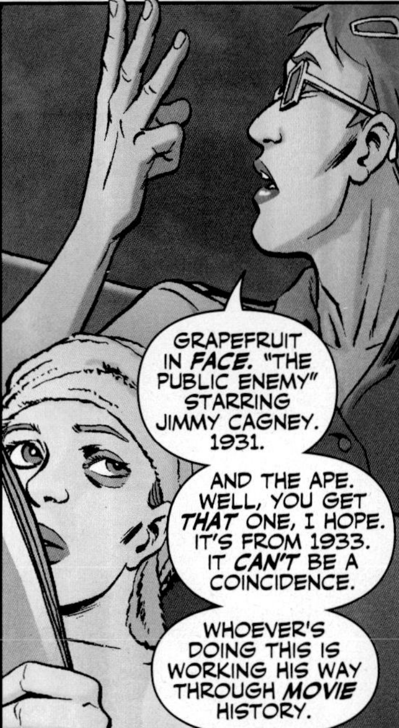

GRAPEFRUIT IN *FACE.* "THE PUBLIC ENEMY" STARRING JIMMY CAGNEY. 1931.
AND THE APE. WELL, YOU GET *THAT* ONE, I HOPE. IT'S FROM 1933. IT *CAN'T* BE A COINCIDENCE.
WHOEVER'S DOING THIS IS WORKING HIS WAY THROUGH *MOVIE* HISTORY.

FILM FREAK.
I WONDER WHAT HE'S GONNA DO *NEXT?*

I APPRECIATE YOUR FILLING THIS ORDER ON SUCH SHORT NOTICE, BILLY.
NO PROBLEM, MY MAN. NOTHING'S TOO GOOD FOR THE GUY WHO SET ME UP WITH A COPY OF THE UNCUT "AMBERSONS." WHERE THE HELL'D YOU FIND IT, ANYWAY?
SOUTH AMERICAN DEALER. HIS STOCK IS IMPRESSIVE-- BUT IT'S NOTHING COMPARED TO YOURS. HE JUST HAS FILMS. YOU HAVE EVERYTHING.
YEAH. THIS PLACE IS LIKE THE LAST SCENE IN "RAIDERS," AIN'T IT?
ACTUALLY, I WAS THINKING OF "CITIZEN KANE."
BEVERLY HILLS
WELL HELL, YOU'D KNOW. YOU LIVE AND BREATHE THOSE WELLES FLICKS, DON'T YOU?
SURE. "KANE," "AMBERSONS," "TOUCH OF EVIL"... THEY'RE ALL MASTERPIECES.
YOUR ORDER'S RIGHT OVER HERE. IT'S NOT COMPLETE, OF COURSE. STILL MISSING THAT CRUCIAL, HARD-TO-FIND ELEMENT.
OF COURSE.
YOU KNOW, BILLY, LATELY I'VE BEEN THINKING ABOUT SHIFTING MY FOCUS. I DON'T WANT TO BE ONE OF THOSE FANS WHO'S OBSESSED WITH NOSTALGIA.
SO WHAT ARE YOU SAYING? ARE YOU GOING TO GO ALL MODERN ON ME, EDISON? ALL CGI, SEQUELS AND FAST-FOOD TIE-INS?
NO. NOTHING THAT EXTREME.
FRAGILE

I'M JUST SKIPPING AHEAD A BIT. LEAVING THE FORTIES AND FIFTIES BEHIND FOR A MORE MODERN ERA.
THE SIXTIES? COOL! YOU MEAN LIKE "EASY RIDER"?
NO.
BLAM
NOT LIKE "EASY RIDER."
I REALIZE IT HAS A CERTAIN CULTURAL SIGNIFICANCE, BUT THAT MOVIE IS EXTREMELY OVERRATED. SELF-INDULGENT, COUNTER-CULTURE DRECK.
I'M THINKING OF A MOVIE FROM THE EARLY SIXTIES. THE IMAGE WAS BEAUTIFUL BLACK AND WHITE, AND THE SATIRE WAS BRACINGLY SHARP.
I'VE LEARNED TO APPRECIATE THOSE QUALITIES IN A FILM. TO EMBRACE THE MORE VIOLENT, MORE NIHILISTIC ASPECTS OF MODERN MOVIES.
AND THAT'S NOT ALL, BILLY. I'VE LEARNED SOMETHING ELSE, TOO.

I'VE LEARNED TO STOP WORRYING...
AND LOVE THE BOMB.

I'M MAD AS HELL, AND I'M NOT GOING TO TAKE IT ANYMORE!
WUAB

WAIT. THAT WASN'T QUITE DRAMATIC ENOUGH. LET ME TRY ANOTHER TAKE.
WUAB

I'M MAD AS HELL, AND I'M NOT GOING TO TAKE IT ANYMORE!
WUAB

THAT'S BETTER.
THE LINE IS FROM "NETWORK," OF COURSE. PETER FINCH WON THE OSCAR FOR PLAYING CRAZED NEWSMAN HOWARD BEALE, BUT DIED BEFORE THE CEREMONY.
WHICH BRINGS ME TO MY REASON FOR COMING INTO YOUR HOMES TONIGHT. YOUR OWN UNTIMELY DEATHS.

I'M NEARING THE LAST SCENE OF MY MOVIE, AND I WANT TO GIVE IT A BIG ENDING. A REALLY BIG ENDING.
THAT MEANS, BECAUSE YOU'RE ALL PART OF THE FILM, YOU'RE CO-STARRING IN THE LAST SCENE, TOO. THE LAST SCENE OF YOUR LIVES.

SORRY, BUT THAT'S HOW IT GOES. IT'S IN THE SCRIPT.
THE PROPS HAVE BEEN PAID FOR. THE LOCATION HAS BEEN SCOUTED AND CHOSEN.

STILL, I'LL GIVE YOU ONE CHANCE FOR A LAST-ACT SAVE. ONE MOVIE TRIVIA QUESTION.
IF YOU CAN FIGURE IT OUT, THE PRIZE IS YOUR LIVES.

HERE IT IS: WHAT DO THE MOVIES "KILLERS FROM SPACE," "RETURN OF THE LIVING DEAD" AND "DR. STRANGELOVE" HAVE IN COMMON?

GOT IT? IT'S A TOUGH ONE, AND I DON'T EXPECT ANY OF YOU REALITY-TV-ADDICTED PHILISTINES TO KNOW THE ANSWER.
THAT'S TOO BAD. A FEW MORE MOVIES UNDER YOUR BELT COULD'VE SAVED YOU ALL.
I NOW RETURN YOU TO YOUR REGULARLY SCHEDULED PROGRAMMING.
GOOD NIGHT...
...AND GOOD LUCK.
THAT WENT WELL. DON'T YOU AGREE, BOBBY?
WHY? WHY, OUT OF EVERYONE HERE, DID YOU LET ME LIVE?
WHY?
BECAUSE YOU'RE THE MOVIE CRITIC, BOBBY.
AND I'M MAKING CINEMA HISTORY.

WHAT THE HELL WAS *THAT?*
TROUBLE.
BIG TROUBLE.

Film Freak. Great. I thought Zatanna's memory zap took care of him.
KARON, YOU'RE THE MOVIE BUFF. ANY IDEA WHAT HE WAS TALKING ABOUT?
WELL, LIKE HE SAID, THE "MAD AS HELL" LINE IS FROM "NETWORK." AND THAT "GOOD NIGHT AND GOOD LUCK"-- THAT WAS FROM CLOONEY'S MOVIE.
NO, I MEAN HIS LITTLE TRIVIA QUIZ. THOSE MOVIES HE MENTIONED. DO THEY HAVE ANYTHING IN COMMON?
THOSE THREE? YOU GOT ME.
ONE'S A 1964 STANLEY KUBRICK CLASSIC, ONE'S AN EIGHTIES ZOM-COM...
ZOMBIE COMEDY.
"ZOM-COM"?
OF COURSE.
BUT THAT THIRD ONE? "KILLERS FROM SPACE"? I'VE NEVER HEARD OF IT.
I HATE THESE GUYS WITH THEIR LITTLE RIDDLES AND CLUES! I DON'T KNOW IF THEY THINK THEY'RE BEING CUTE OR WHAT... THIS GUY, NIGMA... ALL OF THEM!
BUT THIS WAS THAT LATE-NIGHT MOVIE HOST, RIGHT? THE FILM FREAK--?
I WATCH HIS SHOW EVERY WEEK-- OR AT LEAST I DID, 'TIL THEY TOOK IT OFF THE AIR.
YOU KNOW HIM?
YES.
TOO WELL, IN FACT.
AND WHAT'S WORSE...
HE KNOWS ME.

Takes me just five minutes to get to the scene of the crime...
...but I'm already too late.
ANYONE AT THE STATION, SELINA?
SURE. PLENTY OF PEOPLE.
UNFORTUNATELY, VERY FEW OF THEM ARE ALIVE.
AND NONE OF THEM ARE HIM.
I DON'T KNOW WHAT THAT NUTJOB HAS PLANNED, BUT IF THESE ARE THE COMING ATTRACTIONS...
THEN I DON'T WANT TO SEE THE FEATURE PRESENTATION.
JEEZ, SELINA, YOU SOUND JUST LIKE HIM! IF HE'S THAT DANGEROUS-- LET ONE OF THE BIG NAMES HANDLE HIM.
GET SOMEONE FROM THE JUSTICE LEAGUE!
THAT'S WHAT I DID BEFORE, HOLLY. LOOK WHERE IT GOT US.
HMM. THAT'S WEIRD.
WHAT? THE STUDIO FULL OF DEAD PEOPLE? THE MOVIE-OBSESSED PSYCHO?
NO...
ONE OF THE STATION'S VANS IS MISSING...
AND IT'S THE MIDDLE OF THE NIGHT.

THE SILENTS HAD THEIR PURSUITS, OF COURSE, AND MITCHUM'S "THUNDER ROAD" HAD SOME EXCITING SCENES...
BUT THE MOVIE CHASE SCENE-- IN ITS MODERN INCARNATION-- REALLY ARRIVED WITH...
OH, WAIT. YOU'RE GOING TO WANT TO MAKE A LEFT HERE.
GOOD... GOOD...
AS I WAS SAYING, THE MODERN CHASE ARRIVED IN 1968 WITH "BULLITT." STEVE McQUEEN, A MODIFIED MUSTANG AND THE STREETS OF SAN FRANCISCO.
WUAB NEWS
WUAB NEWS
Black
WUAB 3
SCREEEEEECH
NOT MUCH OF A MOVIE, BUT A GROUNDBREAKING CHASE. BUD EKINS, WHO HANDLED THE MUSTANG, WAS AN AMAZING DRIVER.
LEFT AT THIS LIGHT.
m Bobby Schaper
WUAB-43
WUAB
YOU'RE A PRETTY IMPRESSIVE DRIVER YOURSELF, SCHAPER. WOULDN'T HAVE EXPECTED IT FROM A TWELFTH-RATE TV MOVIE CRITIC.
BUT I'M NOT A GREAT DRIVER! I'M NOT EVEN A GOOD DRIVER! I DON'T UNDERSTAND HOW THIS IS HAPPENING!
SCREEEEEECH
THAT, MY FRIEND...
IS THE MAGIC OF MOVIES.

THE MAGIC OF MOVIES? BUT THIS ISN'T A MOVIE! IT'S REAL LIFE!
IS IT?
THEN WHY IS A WOMAN IN A LEATHER CAT COSTUME FOLLOWING US ON A STOLEN MOTORCYCLE?
WHAT? REALLY?
YES, REALLY. THAT'S THE TROUBLE WITH YOU SHALLOW METROPLEX CRITICS.
YOU FORGET THAT ANYTHING CAN HAPPEN IN A MOVIE.
BABY CARRIAGE.
SCREEEEEECH
YAAAAAAH!
KRRASH
LIQUORS
Idiots. I should stop. I should make sure that woman and her baby are okay.
No. Can't. Besides, she looks okay...
I hope.
NOW, THANKS TO THE EFFORTS OF A BEAUTY WITH THE MARQUEE-WORTHY NAME OF ZATANNA, I'M IN A MOVIE. THIS MOVIE.
CATWOMAN'S GAINING ON US! SHE'S GOING TO CATCH US!
DON'T GET YOUR HOPES UP, BOBBY. WE'RE IN "THE FRENCH CONNECTION." BEST PICTURE, 1971. A REVOLUTIONARY CINEMATIC CRIME DRAMA.

"SHE'S LIKE SOMETHING FROM A SEVENTIES DRIVE-IN. PURE EXPLOITATION. OUTLANDISH COSTUME, CHEAP STUNTS. LIKE EVEL KNIEVEL."
DID YOU KNOW THAT IN THE SEVENTIES, THE SO-CALLED GREATEST DECADE OF FILM, THERE WERE TWO-- TWO!-- MOVIES ABOUT HIM?
ORSON WELLES COULDN'T GET A FILM FINANCED TO SAVE HIS LIFE, BUT THAT FLASH IN THE PAN WAS IMMORTALIZED ON CELLULOID NOT ONCE BUT TWICE!
W-WHAT IS THAT?
IT'S A SPECIAL EFFECT, BOBBY. CINEMA IS ALL ABOUT SPECTACLE.
COIPEL-
I SUPPOSE THAT'S WHERE MR. KNIEVEL FITS IN. HE WAS A UNIQUE PERSONALITY. A SINGULAR SCREEN PRESENCE.
WHAT HE DID MAY HAVE LOOKED EASY, BUT IT WASN'T.
AFTER ALL, NOT EVERY-ONE CAN BE A MOTORCYCLE DAREDEVIL.
BOOOM

C'mon...
C'mon...
OKAY OR NO WAY?
Get your
from Bobby
WUAB-43
NNGH!
DO YOU THINK SHE *SURVIVED?*
DOUBTFUL. AT ANY RATE, SHE'S NO LONGER *IMPORTANT* TO THE PLOT. BESIDES, WE'RE MAKING A *BIG* TRANSITION HERE.
IN THIS SCENE, WE CUT FROM *GRITTY* EARLY SEVENTIES CRIME DRAMA...
...TO *CREEPY* LATE SEVENTIES SCI-FI HORROR.
NOW COME ON. THE CAMERAS ARE *ROLLING.*
FREE Kahndaq
13

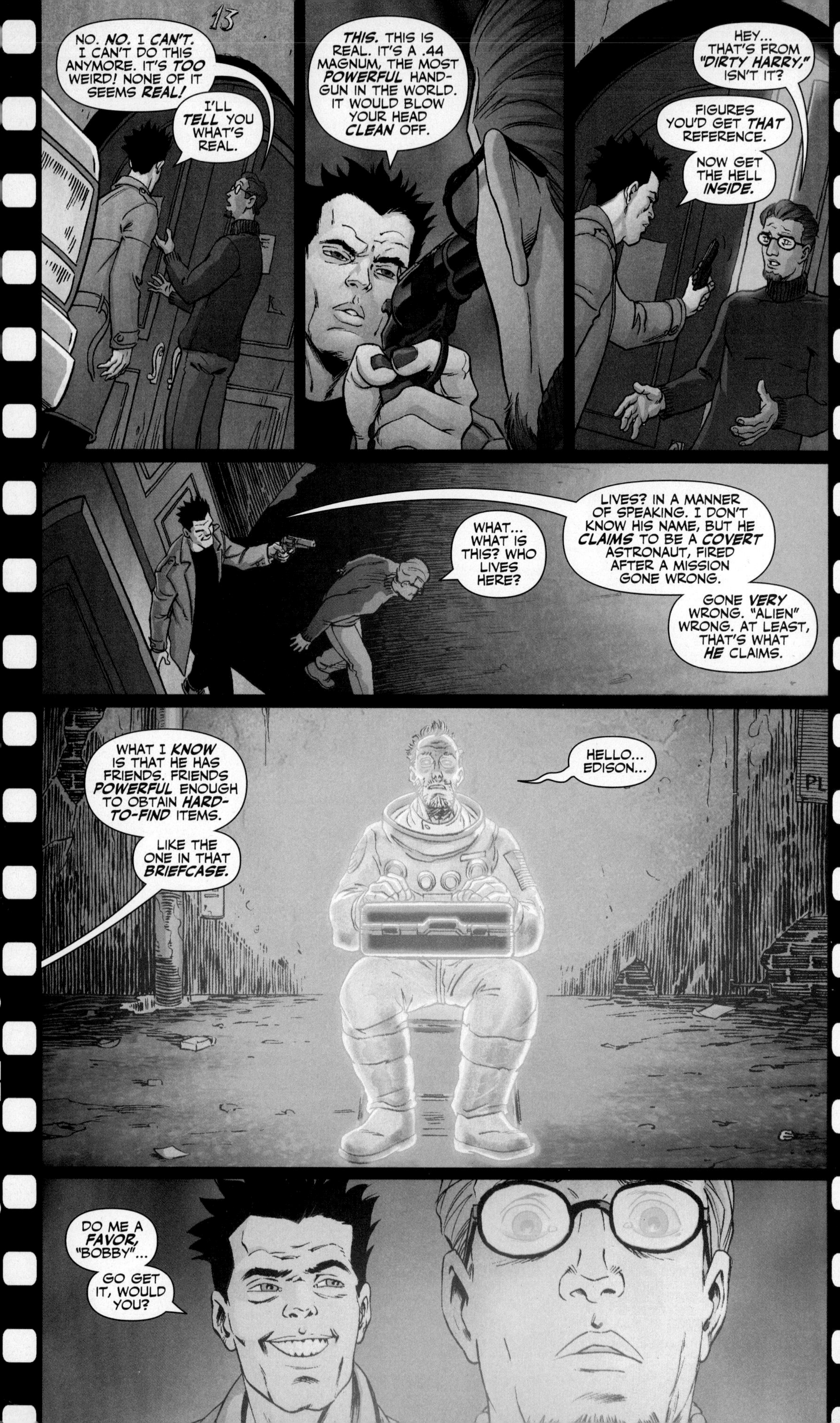
13
NO. NO. I CAN'T. I CAN'T DO THIS ANYMORE. IT'S TOO WEIRD! NONE OF IT SEEMS REAL!
I'LL TELL YOU WHAT'S REAL.
THIS. THIS IS REAL. IT'S A .44 MAGNUM, THE MOST POWERFUL HAND-GUN IN THE WORLD. IT WOULD BLOW YOUR HEAD CLEAN OFF.
HEY... THAT'S FROM "DIRTY HARRY," ISN'T IT?
FIGURES YOU'D GET THAT REFERENCE.
NOW GET THE HELL INSIDE.
WHAT... WHAT IS THIS? WHO LIVES HERE?
LIVES? IN A MANNER OF SPEAKING. I DON'T KNOW HIS NAME, BUT HE CLAIMS TO BE A COVERT ASTRONAUT, FIRED AFTER A MISSION GONE WRONG.
GONE VERY WRONG. "ALIEN" WRONG. AT LEAST, THAT'S WHAT HE CLAIMS.
WHAT I KNOW IS THAT HE HAS FRIENDS. FRIENDS POWERFUL ENOUGH TO OBTAIN HARD-TO-FIND ITEMS.
LIKE THE ONE IN THAT BRIEFCASE.
HELLO... EDISON...
DO ME A FAVOR, "BOBBY"...
GO GET IT, WOULD YOU?

SELINA? ARE YOU OKAY? YOU SOUND AWFUL!
I FEEL AWFUL. BUT I'M ALIVE, AT LEAST FOR THE MOMENT. I'M PRETTY BANGED UP, THOUGH. MIGHT NEED YOUR HELP BEFORE THIS IS THROUGH.
DID KARON EVER FIGURE OUT THAT RIDDLE? THE ONE FILM FREAK WAS BLATHERING ABOUT?
SORT OF. SHE DOWNLOADED A COPY OF "KILLERS FROM SPACE" AND SHE'S BEEN FAST-FORWARDING THROUGH IT.
HOW IS IT, KARON?
TERRIBLE. AND THE ENDING IS THE WORST PART.
OUR HERO STANDS IN FRONT OF A GENTLY FLUTTERING VENETIAN BLIND AS ATOMIC BOMBS EXPLODE OUTSIDE.
IT'S AS DOPEY AS THE NUCLEAR FINALE OF "LIVING DEAD" IS FUNNY, OR THE APOCALYPTIC END OF "STRANGELOVE" IS...
OH MY GOD. I KNOW WHAT HE'S GOING TO DO.
Well, it's a big finish, I'll give him that.
Now the only question is do I seek medical help for the internal injuries I've probably got, or jump down there and follow them?
No choice, really.
None at all.
HURRY UP, SCHAPER. THE CLOCK IS TICKING.
YOU DON'T WANT TO BE LATE FOR YOUR BIG SCENE.
FREE Kahndaq
I just hope I don't pass out.

WHAT ARE WE DOING? WHAT DID YOU GET FROM THAT... THAT MAN?
EXACTLY WHAT WE NEEDED. THE MOVIE IS ALMOST OVER. THE CLIMAX IS JUST AROUND THE CORNER.
WUAB3
IT'S A SURPRISE. LIKE LUKE SKYWALKER'S PARENTAGE. IT CAN'T BE REVEALED UNTIL EXACTLY THE RIGHT MOMENT.
I... I THINK I NEED TO PULL OVER. ALL OF A SUDDEN, I FEEL AWFUL. LIKE I'M GOING TO PASS OUT.
IT'S PROBABLY RADIATION POISONING. YOU KNOW, FROM THAT URANIUM-235 YOU CARRIED OUT TO THE VAN.
WHAT?
DON'T WORRY.
THAT SORT OF THING TAKES YEARS TO KILL YOU.
V LEW N
M S
AL LE
AND BESIDES, WE'RE HERE.
NOW HELP ME GET THIS INSIDE.
I HAVE A FEELING THE PLOT TWISTS ARE ABOUT TO START HAPPENING ANY SECOND.
WUAB

THEY SURE DON'T MAKE MOVIE PALACES LIKE THIS ANYMORE. IT'S LIKE A CATHEDRAL TO CINEMA. IT'S A SHAME WE'RE GOING TO...
URK... URK...
JUST PUT IT THERE, IN THE CENTER OF THE STAGE. AND FOR GOD'S SAKE, BE CAREFUL!
I... I'VE DONE EVERYTHING YOU ASKED. PLEASE, LET ME GET OUT OF HERE BEFORE THE FINAL SCENE...
EDISON?
SORRY, BOBBY.
YOU'RE LIKE A COP WITH A DAY TO GO 'TIL RETIREMENT.
YOU DON'T LIVE TO SEE THE END CREDITS.
BLAM
BUT YOU'RE A MOVIE CRITIC.
YOU KNOW HOW IT IS.

A gunshot?
Passed out. Stupid! Stupid!

Whatever he's doing, he's doing it now.

Ow. This is not going to be easy.
It might require reinforcements.

HOLLY? I'M GOING TO NEED YOU AT THE EASTERLY ASAP.
SPARE MASK AND GLOVES ARE IN THE CLOSET. SUIT UP AND BE READY FOR ANYTHING.

Now I just hope I'm not late for my last minute save...

Damn. Holly's right.
I do sound just like that lunatic.

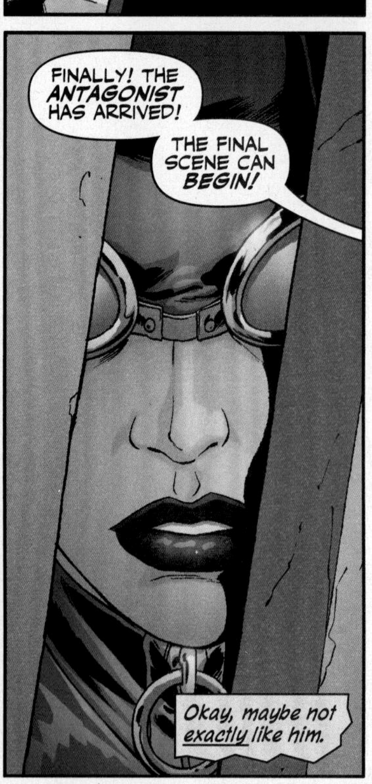
FINALLY! THE ANTAGONIST HAS ARRIVED!
THE FINAL SCENE CAN BEGIN!
Okay, maybe not exactly like him.

HOW DO YOU *LIKE* IT? SORT OF A GREATEST HITS MONTAGE. IT'S AMAZING HOW MANY MOVIES MAKE USE OF A *MUSHROOM CLOUD* MOTIF.

OF COURSE, MOST OF IT'S *STOCK* FOOTAGE-- A-BOMB TESTS, DESERT EXPLOSIONS, THAT SORT OF THING.

STILL, IT'S AN *IMPRESSIVE* SIGHT, ISN'T IT? BUT DON'T JUST STARE UP AT THE *SCREEN*...

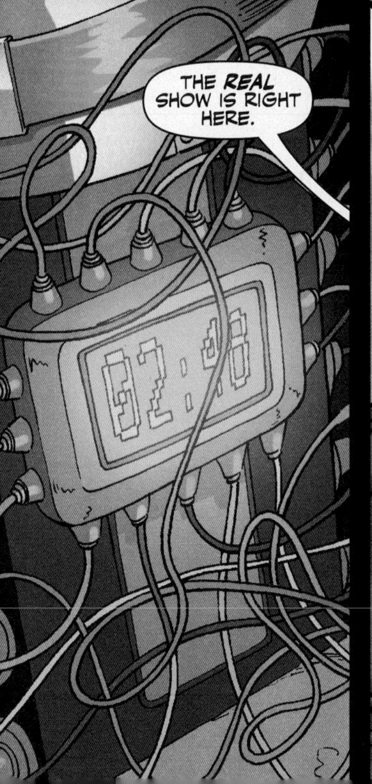

THE *REAL* SHOW IS RIGHT HERE.

AND *THIS* ISN'T STOCK FOOTAGE, CGI, ANIMATION OR TRICK PHOTOGRAPHY...

IT'S THE *GENUINE* ARTICLE. CINEMA *VÉRITÉ*.
ALERT THE *ACADEMY*. MY MOVIE IS NOW A *DOCUMENTARY*. A DOCUMENTARY ABOUT THE DEATH OF A *WHOLE* LOT OF PEOPLE.

I KNOW WHAT YOU'VE GOT PLANNED, EDISON. IT'S NOT GOING TO WORK. GIVE ME THE DETONATOR. THIS ISN'T HOW YOU WANT TO END THINGS.
YOU'RE WRONG. THIS IS EXACTLY HOW I WANT TO END THINGS. AND ADMIT IT...
IT'S HOW YOU WANT THEM TO END, TOO.
I DON'T KNOW WHO YOU ARE UNDER THAT MASK, BUT YOU OBVIOUSLY HAVE A FLAIR FOR THE DRAMATIC...
DO YOU REALLY WANT TO DIE LONG PAST YOUR PRIME? OR DO YOU WANT TO DIE NOW, AT YOUR PEAK, IN AN UNFORGETTABLE MOVIE MOMENT?
MARLON BRANDO OR JAMES DEAN. PRETTY EASY CHOICE, ISN'T IT?
IT SURE IS. MAKE MINE MARLON.
NOW GIVE ME THE DAMN DETONATOR.
DETONATOR? THERE'S NO DETONATOR.
JUST A NUCLEAR BOMB AND A TICKING CLOCK. YOU'VE SEEN IT IN A MILLION MOVIES.
02:17
AND ALL THOSE MOVIES ASK THE SAME CRUCIAL QUESTION: THERE ARE A LOT OF WIRES IN THERE, CATWOMAN...
WHICH ONE DO YOU CUT TO SAVE THE DAY?

BUT DON'T BOTHER TRYING TO FIGURE IT *OUT*, CATWOMAN. THERE'S NO TIME LEFT. THE ENDING-- THE *PERFECT* ENDING-- IS ALMOST UPON US.

I MEAN, REALLY. AFTER DROPPING A *BUILDING* ON TWO POLICEMEN AND LETTING A GIANT *APE* LOOSE, WHAT ELSE COULD I DO? I HAD TO FINISH BIG-- *REALLY* BIG.

THE LAST SCENE IN THIS MOVIE-- IN *MY* MOVIE-- WILL HAVE PEOPLE TALKING FOR DECADES. IT'S THE KIND OF THING THAT WILL *NEVER* BE FORGOTTEN!
ISN'T *THAT* WORTH DYING FOR?

BESIDES, IT'S NOT THE END OF THE *WORLD*. IT'S JUST THE END OF THE *MOVIE.*
AND, ADMITTEDLY, THE END OF *GOTHAM.*

LIKE GEORGE C. SCOTT SAID IN *"STRANGELOVE"*...
"I'M NOT SAYING WE WOULDN'T GET OUR *HAIR* MUSSED. BUT I DO SAY NO MORE THAN 10 TO 20 MILLION KILLED, *TOPS."*

"DEPENDING ON THE *BREAKS."*
That does it.

STOP IT WITH THOSE STUPID MOVIE QUOTES!
"MOTHER OF MERCY..."
"IS THIS THE END OF..."
SHUT UP! SHUT UP! SHUT UP!
THWACK
YOU'RE NOT MAKING A MOVIE! THERE AREN'T ANY CAMERAS-- OR SETS-- OR ACTORS!
"MADE IT, MA...."
SLAM SLAM SLAM
UHHH... "...TOP OF THE WORLD..."
IT'S JUST YOU-- JUST ANOTHER GOTHAM LUNATIC--
SITTING ALONE IN THE DARK!
WHAM

YOU SICK LITTLE BASTARD! SPOUTING LINES OF DIALOGUE WHILE YOU KILL MILLIONS OF PEOPLE?
YOU WANT A MOVIE QUOTE? I'LL GIVE YOU A MOVIE QUOTE.

"THAT'S ALL, FOLKS."

KRUNCH
GEEK.

SELINA! ARE YOU OKAY? WHAT HAPPENED HERE?
NOTHING COMPARED TO WHAT'S GOING TO HAPPEN IF I DON'T DISARM THIS THING WITHIN THE NEXT TWENTY SECONDS.
IS THAT REALLY A...
IT SURE IS.
BUT... BUT HOW DO YOU KNOW WHICH WIRE TO CUT?
HOW DO YOU KNOW WHICH ONE IS THE RIGHT ONE?
SELINA?
SNIP!
THEY'RE ALL THE RIGHT ONE. CUTTING ANY WIRE WILL SHUT IT DOWN.
DON'T BELIEVE EVERY-THING YOU SEE IN THE MOVIES, HOLLY.
THIS IS THE REAL WORLD.

SO WAIT... HE DIDN'T KNOW WHO YOU REALLY ARE?
APPARENTLY NOT. WHATEVER ELSE ZATANNA SCREWED UP WITH THAT SPELL OF HERS-- AND SHE SCREWED UP A LOT-- SHE AT LEAST GOT THAT RIGHT.

SO WHAT'S NEXT?
NEXT? I CHECK ON HELENA, SLIP OUT OF THIS COSTUME AND SLEEP FOR A DAY OR SO.
SOUNDS LIKE A PLAN.

IS THAT BLOOD?

NO... NOT AGAIN...

KARON! WHAT'S HAPPENING? IS HELENA ALL RIGHT?

SURE... SHE'S FINE... IT'S JUST THAT...

HE GOT HERE A FEW MINUTES AGO. I WASN'T SURE WHAT TO DO...

HE SAID HE JUST WANTED TO HOLD HIS...

HIS...
...HIS GRANDDAUGHTER.

WE NEED TO TALK, SELINA.
"YOU'RE RIGHT, SLAM. THERE ARE THINGS YOU NEED TO KNOW.
"ABOUT ME...
"ABOUT SAM...
"ABOUT BOTH OF US.
"WHAT HAPPENED TO HIM...
"AND ME...
"AND... WELL..."
Pregnant

SO, EVEN THOUGH, AFTER BREAKING HOLLY OUT OF JAIL, SUBDUING A GIANT APE, AND STOPPING THE EAST END FROM BECOMING A RADIOACTIVE RUIN...
...THERE'S NOTHING I'D RATHER DO THAN TAKE THE WORLD'S LONGEST NAP...
YOU'RE RIGHT. WE DO NEED TO TALK.
BUT I THINK YOU'RE GOING TO WANT TO SIT DOWN FIRST, SLAM.
BECAUSE THIS...
...THIS GETS A LITTLE COMPLICATED.

HEY, KID. GET ME A DRINK, WOULD YOU? SCOTCH. NEAT.
I'VE BEEN THINKING A LOT LATELY. ABOUT WHEN EXACTLY EVERY-THING WENT SO CRAZY...
NEAT?
JUST A SHOT. NO WATER, NO ICE.
AND I'VE NARROWED IT DOWN TO THE SPLIT SECOND...
UH, I DON'T KNOW IF THAT'S SUCH A GOOD IDEA, SLAM...
TO THE EXACT MOMENT WHEN I PULLED THAT TRIGGER...
JUST BRING ME THE DAMN BOTTLE, HOLLY.
AND KILLED BLACK MASK.
YOU DID WHAT?!?
KERRASH

THAT'S WHAT THEY ARRESTED *ME* FOR! I THOUGHT THAT COP WAS *CRAZY!*

BUT HE WAS *RIGHT!?* CATWOMAN REALLY *DID* MURDER BLACK MASK? FOR GOD'S SAKE, SELINA, WHY DIDN'T YOU *TELL* ME?

I *COULDN'T* TELL YOU, HOLLY. I COULDN'T TELL *ANYBODY.* THE STAKES WERE JUST *WAY* TOO HIGH.

I...
I...
I *PROTECTED* YOU FROM THE POLICE. I *LIED* FOR YOU. BUT YOU...

YOUR *FRIEND?* HER GIRLFRIEND? THE *DETECTIVE* AND HIS COP KID?
THEY DIE PAINFULLY.

I DID WHAT I *HAD* TO DO, HOLLY. I'M NOT *PROUD...*
BUT I'M NOT *ASHAMED,* EITHER.

YOU SHOULD UNDERSTAND, HOLLY. MORE THAN ANYONE ELSE.

"SOMETIMES YOU HAVE TO TAKE A LIFE...
"TO SAVE A LIFE."

HOLLY... WHAT DID YOU DO?
...SAVED YOU... FOR ONCE...

SHE'S RIGHT, KID. WE ALL HAVE OUR REASONS.

YES, I DID. SO DID SAM.
WE... WE BOTH DID. REASONS FOR EVERYTHING HAPPENED. THE FIGHTS, THE FIRE...
...ALL EXCEPT FOR HELENA.

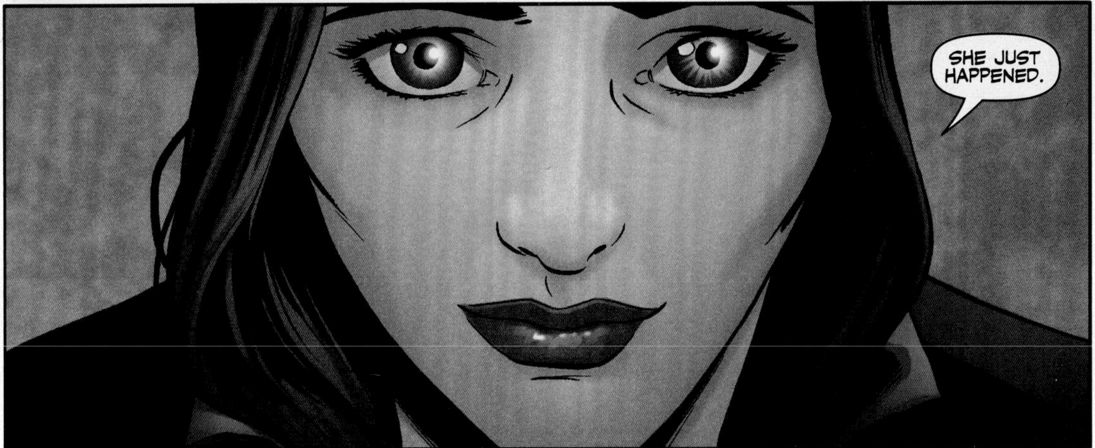
SHE JUST HAPPENED.

SAM? HE'S THE...?
BUT I THOUGHT, I MEAN, YOU AND SLAM WERE ALWAYS...
IT'S OKAY, KID. SAM TOLD ME. WELL, HE TOLD ME EVERYTHING HE COULD.
NOW, SELINA, YOU TELL ME. FILL IN THE BLANKS.

"WHY DID IT HAPPEN, KIDDO? WAS I TOO OLD? TOO BROKEN DOWN? DID YOU REALIZE YOU DIDN'T WANT BRADLEY SENIOR...
"AND DECIDE TO GO WITH THE NEWER MODEL?"

THAT WASN'T IT AT ALL. LIKE I SAID, IT'S COMPLICATED.
AND BELIEVE ME, A YEAR AGO, WHEN THIS ALL GOT STARTED...

"...LOOKS HAD NOTHING TO DO WITH IT."
I FEEL RIDICULOUS.
YOU LOOK GREAT. REALLY.

IT'S LOW-TECH, IT'S RETRO, IT'S URBAN, AND MOST IMPORTANT, IT'S DARK AND COVERS YOUR FACE. THAT'S WHAT YOU NEED IN THIS LINE OF WORK, SAM.
YOU DON'T HAVE THE BADGE ANYMORE. YOU CAN'T HAVE PEOPLE KNOWING WHO YOU ARE.
WE MIGHT BE FIGHTING CRIME, BUT WE'RE STILL BREAKING THE LAW.
THIS ISN'T GOING TO FOOL ANYONE. THEY'LL GUESS RIGHT AWAY WHO I AM UNDER THIS GETUP.
IN GOTHAM? ARE YOU KIDDING?
EVEN WITH THE BAT AND THE BOY WONDER OUT OF THE PICTURE, THERE ARE STILL TOO MANY MASKS FOR ANYONE TO KEEP TRACK.
TRUST ME. YOU'LL FIT RIGHT IN.
NOW C'MON...
THE NIGHT IS YOUNG, AND SO ARE WE.
LET'S DO SOME GOOD.
"AND WE DID."

KERRASH
"SAM WAS A NATURAL. I HAVE NO IDEA HOW GOOD HE WAS WITH A BADGE...
"BUT WITHOUT ONE, HE WAS A DYNAMO.
"BLACK MASK WAS DEAD, BUT HIS EMPIRE LIVED ON...
POW
THOK
"...UNTIL WE PUT IT OUT OF BUSINESS...
"BIT BY BIT BY BIT.
"METH LABS.
"CHOP SHOPS.
"VICE DENS OF VARIOUS SHAPES AND SIZES.
"WE SHUT THEM ALL DOWN.
"JUST THE TWO OF US."

"OF COURSE, ALL THAT WORK... ALL THOSE DEALERS AND BOOSTERS AND *CHEMISTS* AND SNEAK THIEVES AND PIMPS AND *PUSHERS*...
"THEY WEREN'T WHO WE WERE *REALLY* AFTER.
26
G.C.P.D.

"WE NEEDED TO GET THEM TO GET TO OUR *ACTUAL* TARGET... BLACK MASK'S FORMER RIGHT-HAND MAN...*
"A YUPPIE SON OF A BITCH NAMED *DYLAN*.
*SEE THE CATWOMAN: *RELENTLESS* TRADE PAPERBACK.

"*HE* WAS THE ONE WHO ORDERED THAT HOSPITAL *HIT* ON SAM..."
HAVE THEM KILL HIM.
AND HAVE THEM MAKE A MESS DOING IT.

"AND SAM WANTED TO PAY HIM BACK. IN *SPADES*."
WHAT HE DID TO ME... TO YOU. WHAT HE DID TO MY *DAD*.
IT CAN'T GO ON. I MEAN, SOMEONE'S GOT TO PUT AN END TO IT, ONCE AND FOR ALL.

AT FIRST, SO DID *I*.
BUT I RECONSIDERED.

YOU WERE *RIGHT*, HOLLY. THAT'S THE LINE WE DON'T CROSS. JUST BECAUSE WE DID IT ONCE DOESN'T MEAN WE DO IT AGAIN.
SO I CONVINCED SAM WE COULD TAKE HIM DOWN *ANOTHER* WAY.
DESTROY THE OPERATION. GET HIS GOONS TO TALK. TO FINGER DYLAN.

"THE NIGHT WE GOT HIM-- I MEAN FINALLY GOT HIM-- WELL, I CAN'T EXPLAIN EXACTLY HOW OR WHY IT HAPPENED.
"MAYBE IT WAS THE ADRENALINE..."
SKRRAKKSHH
"MAYBE IT WAS THE COSTUMES...
"HELL, MAYBE IT WAS THE VIOLENCE.
EVIDENCE
"WHATEVER IT WAS...
"THAT NIGHT..."
POLICE
NICE WORK, SELINA.
RIGHT BACK ATCHA.

"...WE CONNECTED."

"WE ONLY CONNECTED LIKE *THAT* ONCE.
"...JUST *ONCE.*
"BUT THAT'S *ALL* IT TAKES.
"LOOKING BACK, THAT NIGHT PROBABLY SEEMS MORE PERFECT THAN IT *REALLY* WAS...
"BUT THAT'S BECAUSE WHEN IT WAS *OVER,* EVERYTHING WENT SO WRONG... SO *FAST.*"

"A WEEK LATER, DYLAN WAS *BACK* ON THE STREET, THANKS TO A VERY *EXPENSIVE* LAWYER ARGUING FOR A VERY *INEXPENSIVE* BAIL.
"SOMEHOW, HE RAN INTO *SAM*... OR VICE VERSA..."
BRADLEY. GET IN.
NOW.
SFDK
"I'M NOT REALLY SURE *WHAT* HAPPENED.

AND IF I DON'T?
DO YOU SEE THAT *PLAYGROUND* OVER THERE?
"*NO* ONE IS."

I'LL HAVE MY DRIVER EMPTY HIS *UZI* IN ITS DIRECTION.
YOU IN THIS CAR OR THE *KIDS* IN A HEARSE. YOUR CHOICE.

NO CHOICE.
GOOD.

WHAT SAY WE GO OVER TO *MY* PLACE?

POW
YOU REALLY THOUGHT THAT COSTUME WOULD FOOL ME? WOULD FOOL ANYBODY?
YOU KILLED TWO OF MY MEN. I KNOW WHO YOU ARE, BRADLEY. NO MATTER WHAT YOU'RE WEARING.
I WORKED FOR BLACK MASK FOR YEARS, BRADLEY. RAN HIS ERRANDS. LISTENED TO HIS STUPID JOKES. IT WASN'T EASY, BUT HE TAUGHT ME A LOT.
MOST OF ALL, HE TAUGHT ME TO TIE UP LOOSE ENDS.
KRUNCH
YOU'VE CAUSED ME A LOT OF TROUBLE, BRADLEY, YOU AND THAT FRIEND OF YOURS. SHUT DOWN MY OPERATIONS, GOT ME THROWN IN JAIL. AND WORSE.
AND HER? TOSS ME FROM A MOVING TRAIN? BREAK MY NOSE? SHE'LL PAY FOR WHAT SHE'S DONE. PAY DEARLY.
YOU SON OF A...
GO AHEAD. SPEAK. AND DON'T WORRY ABOUT BEING LOUD, EITHER THE TOP FIVE FLOOR OF THIS BUILDING ARE MINE. AND THEY'RE EMPTY.
NO ONE IS GOING TO HEAR US...
NO MATTER HOW LOUD...
GAAAAH!!
BLAM
...OUR CONVERSATION GETS.
NNNGH!
BLAM

LEAVE. I'LL HANDLE THINGS FROM HERE.
NNNNG... OH, GOD...
YOU SURE, MR. DYLAN?
I'M SURE.

NOW, BRADLEY, IF YOU'LL EXCUSE ME, I HAVE TO MAKE A PHONE CALL...
MAY I BORROW YOUR PHONE?
GGGHH!

JUDGING BY THE NUMBER OF LATE-NIGHT CALLS TO AND FROM "SELINA," SHE MUST BE SOMEONE SPECIAL.
SOMEONE VERY SPECIAL.

MAYBE EVEN SPECIAL ENOUGH TO SLIP INTO A LEATHER CATSUIT AND RUN AROUND THE ROOFTOPS, EH?
WELL, WE'LL FIND OUT SOON ENOUGH.

I'M INVITING HER OVER.

"I WAS OUT THAT NIGHT...

"I HAD TO CHECK SOMETHING."
OKAY, LET'S SEE...
TWO PLUS SIGNS MEANS...
Pregnant

OH, BOY.

BREET BREET

SAM?
NO. BUT I'M CALLING ON HIS BEHALF.
IF YOU'D LIKE TO SEE HIM ALIVE, I SUGGEST YOU JOIN US. YOU'RE FAMILIAR WITH THE ADDRESS, I'M SURE.

YOU WERE HERE A FEW WEEKS AGO.
VISITING BLACK MASK.

SHE'S ON HER WAY. OF COURSE, WHEN SHE GETS WITHIN A BLOCK OF THIS BUILDING, A SNIPER'S BULLET IN HER SPINE WILL TAKE THE FIGHT OUT OF HER.
I STILL HAVEN'T DECIDED WHICH ONE OF YOU TO KILL FIRST.

DO I MAKE YOU WATCH ME KILL HER, OR VICE VERSA?
I SUPPOSE IT DOESN'T MATTER. YOU'LL BOTH BE DEAD. THEN YOUR FATHER WILL FOLLOW.
NO CLEVER RESPONSE? YOU WERE QUITE WITTY A WEEK AGO. SOMETHING WRONG?

HAVE IT YOUR WAY. I DON'T...
SNF SNF
WHAT'S THAT...?

SSSSSSSSSS

FLIK

BOOOM

"IT WASN'T *FAR* FROM MY PLACE.

"BUT I WAS *TOO* LATE.
"*WAY* TOO LATE."

"I KNEW THERE WAS NO WAY SAM COULD SURVIVE.
"THE FIRE, THE FALL, ALL OF IT. IT WAS TOO MUCH.
"BUT THAT DOESN'T MEAN I WASN'T GOING TO TRY TO SAVE HIM.
"I HAD TO.
"I HAD TO TELL HIM."
OH, GOD, SAM... SAM, YOU CAN'T DIE! YOU CAN'T...
UHHH...
I...
I'M GOING TO HAVE A BABY. YOUR BABY.
NOW YOU'LL BE SAFE...
...BOTH OF YOU...

YOU KNOW WHAT HAPPENED *NEXT.* THE INVESTIGATIONS. THE HEADLINES. THE *FUNERAL.*
I'M STILL NOT SURE *WHAT* SAM DID, BUT I'M SURE HE DIED A *HERO.*

SAM... JEEZ, SELINA, WHY DIDN'T YOU JUST *TELL* US? WHY KEEP IT A *MYSTERY?!?*
I WAS THINKING IT COULD BE *ANYONE.* EVEN...YOU KNOW...

BATMAN? PLEASE.
I *DIDN'T* TELL YOU, HOLLY, BECAUSE I DIDN'T TELL *ANYONE.* AFTER SEEING SAM DIE, ALL I COULD THINK ABOUT WAS KEEPING OUR *BABY* SAFE.
BESIDES, I KNEW *THAT* SORT OF REVELATION WOULD BE TOUGH FOR *SOME* PEOPLE TO HEAR.

BUT *YOU* KNEW, SLAM. HE *TOLD* YOU, DIDN'T HE? OR YOU *FIGURED* IT OUT.
IS *THAT* WHY YOU'VE BEEN SO... SO...

HEH.
IT'S BEEN QUITE A YEAR FOR *ME* TOO, SELINA.
QUITE A YEAR.

YOU GET TORTURED AND LEFT FOR *DEAD* BY A SKULL-FACED S.O.B, THEN FIND OUT YOUR *KID* IS WITH THE WOMAN YOU...
WELL...

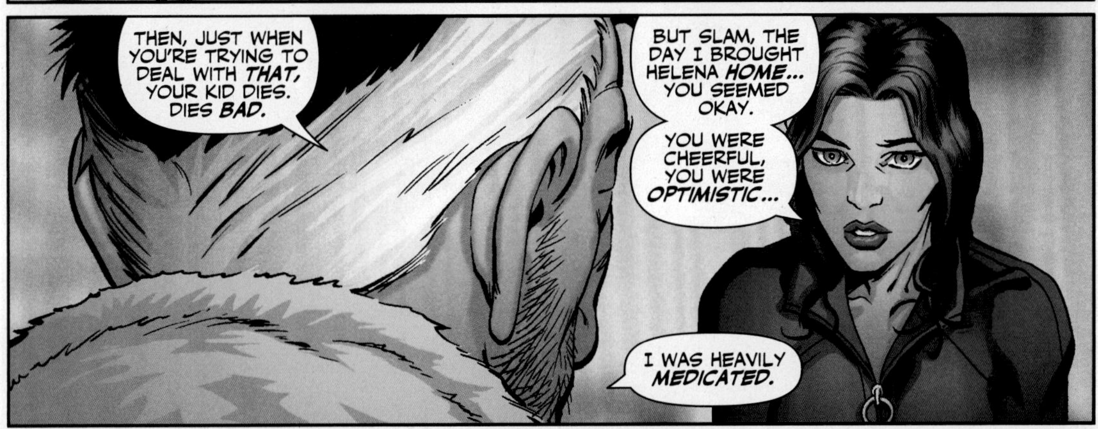
THEN, JUST WHEN YOU'RE TRYING TO DEAL WITH *THAT,* YOUR KID DIES. DIES *BAD.*
BUT SLAM, THE DAY I BROUGHT HELENA *HOME...* YOU SEEMED OKAY.
YOU WERE CHEERFUL, YOU WERE *OPTIMISTIC...*
I WAS HEAVILY *MEDICATED.*

I'M AN *OLD* MAN, SELINA. A YEAR AFTER MY HOSPITAL STAY, I WAS *STILL* TAKING A PAINKILLER COCKTAIL TO K.O AN ELEPHANT...
THEN THE PRESCRIPTION RAN *OUT.*
SO I DECIDED TO *SELF* MEDICATE.

BUT YOU FINALLY BEIN' STRAIGHT WITH ME, KIDDO. AND *ME* BEING STRAIGHT WITH *YOU.*
MAYBE IT'S GONNA STOP ME FROM HITTING *ROCK* BOTTOM.

YOU KNOW, SLAM. YOU NEVER *TOUCHED* YOUR DRINK.
MAYBE YOU'RE ON YOUR WAY BACK *UP.*
SPEAKING OF UP, LOOK WHO'S *AWAKE.* GUESS WE'VE BEEN TALKING ALL NIGHT.

COME HERE, BABE. COME TO MAMA.
SHE REALLY IS A CUTIE.
DAMN RIGHT SHE IS.
YOU KNOW, I NEVER NOTICED IT BEFORE, BUT SHE HAS SAM'S... SHE HAS HER DAD'S NOSE.
THAT'S NOT ALL, SLAM.
SHE HAS HER GRANDPA'S EYES.

SO... SAM.
HE'S HELENA'S *FATHER,* HUH?
She's been waiting to talk about it for days.
I can tell.

THAT'S RIGHT.
I GOTTA TELL YOU, SELINA, I'M *STILL* TRYING TO GET MY HEAD AROUND THAT ONE.

JOIN THE CLUB. IT HAPPENED *FAST* AND IT ENDED *FASTER.*
I KNOW EVERY-ONE EXPECTED HELENA'S DAD TO BE SOMEONE ELSE, SOMEONE MORE *COLORFUL...*
BUT SAM WAS A *GREAT* GUY. EVEN IF HE DIDN'T WEAR A COSTUME. EVEN IF HE *DIDN'T* HAVE ANY POWERS.

I KNOW, SELINA. I KNOW.
SO WHY'D YOU NAME HER "HELENA"? WHY NOT NAME HER SOMETHING LIKE "SAMANTHA"? YOU KNOW, SO HE'D BE REMEMBERED?

DON'T WORRY. HE'S BEING REMEMBERED.
NOW GET FOCUSED. OUR BAIT HAS ARRIVED.

SELINA, THIS REALLY *IS* CRUEL.

A LARGE HAM AND PINEAPPLE AND WE'RE *NOT* EVEN GOING TO GET TO *EAT* IT?

FINE. BECAUSE BESIDES BEING *RIGHT* ABOUT THE COPS NOT CARING ABOUT ME ANYMORE, I'M ALSO HUNGRY. *DAMN* HUNGRY.

DON'T WORRY.

THE *$500 TIP* HE'S GOING TO GET WILL SMOOTH OVER ANY *HURT* FEELINGS.

SORRY, HOLLY.

THAT'S *NOT* WHY I ORDERED IT.

I KNOW, I KNOW. YOU ORDERED IT TO PROVE A *POINT*. AND I STILL SAY YOU'RE WRONG.

IF I AM, HOLLY, I'LL BUY YOU *ANOTHER* PIZZA ON THE WAY HOME.

AND I STILL THINK IT'S *MEAN* TO DRAG THIS POOR DRONE INTO YOUR LITTLE EXPERIMENT. HE'S *JUST* THE PIZZA GUY.

GAAAAAH!
WHAT THE HELL?!? WHAT THE HELL?!?
THIS IS WHAT THE HELL.
SATISFIED?
LIEUTENANT
GOTHAM CITY
NOW IT'S MY TURN TO ASK "WHAT THE HELL."
LIKE WHAT THE HELL ARE YOU DOING HERE? WHAT THE HELL IS YOUR CONNECTION TO THE WOMAN WHO LIVES HERE?
WHAT THE HELL DO YOU KNOW ABOUT CATWOMAN?
CATWOMAN?! LISTEN, I'M JUST DELIVERING A PIZZA.
OR AT LEAST I WAS.
MAYBE. MAYBE. I'LL BE WATCHING YOU, PIZZA BOY. SO YOU WATCH YOUR ASS.
CRAZY COP! I'M GONNA SUE YOU, I'M GONNA SUE THE CITY, I'M GONNA SUE THE MAYOR, I'M GONNA--

AND *THAT,* HOLLY...
IS WHY YOU *CAN'T* GO HOME AGAIN.
$100
COUNTER
OFFICE

BUT LENAHAN'S JUST *ONE* COP, SELINA. JUST ONE *CRAZY* COP. I DON'T EVEN THINK ANYONE ELSE ON THE FORCE *CARES*.
DOESN'T MATTER, KIDDO.
AS LONG AS YOUR NAME IS *LINKED* TO CATWOMAN, YOU'RE GOING TO BE ON THEIR *RADAR*.
LOW FLYING, BUT STILL A *BLIP* ON THEIR SCREEN.
THERE'S *ALWAYS* GOING TO BE SOME COP SOMEWHERE, LOOKING TO MAKE A NAME FOR HIMSELF.

HE'LL BE SURFING THROUGH THE *COMPUTER* ONE DAY, SPOT YOUR NAME AND FIGURE BAGGING *CATWOMAN* IS AS GOOD A WAY AS ANY TO GET AHEAD.
WAIT A SECOND.

WHAT THE...?
OOPS! SORRY!

FIRST SOME CRAZY *COP*, NOW *THIS*? WHAT? DO I HAVE A *SIGN* ON MY BACK OR SOMETHING?
SO, ANYWAY...

CAN'T YOU JUST, YOU KNOW, GO INTO THE COMPUTER AND WIPE *OUT* ALL THAT INFO? *ERASE* ME SOMEHOW?
I DON'T KNOW, HOLLY. THAT'S A *LITTLE* OUT OF MY LEAGUE.
AM I SOME SORT OF TACKLING--
EH?

BUT I'M *WORKING* ON IT, HOLLY...
I'M WORKING ON IT.
HOLY...

THAT NIGHT...
SOMEWHERE IN ALASKA...
SOMEWHERE SECRET...
FINE, SIDNEY, FINE. MARIA IS IN HER THIRD YEAR AT MOSCOW STATE, AND LITTLE ANYA IS TAKING GYMNASTICS. THEY GROW UP SO FAST!
DON'T I KNOW IT. JAMES GRADUATES FROM YALE NEXT SPRING. WELL, BE SURE TO GIVE THEM MY BEST, YURI.
NOW, I SUPPOSE WE'D BETTER GET DOWN TO BUSINESS.
DA. NEITHER YOUR GOVERNMENT NOR MINE WOULD LOOK FAVORABLY ON THIS EXCHANGE MAKING THE NEWS.
SO LET'S SEE... I'VE BROUGHT THIRTEEN COVERT U.S. OPERATIVES SPORTING AN ASSORTMENT OF MUSCULAR MODIFICATIONS.
AND YOU'VE BROUGHT...?
JUST TWO.
URK... URK...
AH YES. BORIS AND NATASHA ULYANOV. CODE-NAMED "HAMMER" AND "SICKLE."
A PAIR OF AMUSING RELICS FROM THE LAST DAYS OF THE SOVIET EMPIRE.
URRRK!

HEY...
WHAT'S WITH ALL THAT--
URRKK
SPINK
WHAM
GOOD, BORIS. GOOD.
STOP HIM! STOP HIM!
NOW FREE ME.
DA.
IGNORE THEM, BORIS.
THEY DON'T MATTER. NOT ANYMORE.
BLAMBLAMBLAM
BLAMBLAMBLA
BLAMBLAMBLA

THOSE RESTRAINTS WERE SUPPOSED TO *HOLD* THEM! WE BUILT THEM TO *YOUR* SPECS! HOW IS HE *DOING* THAT?!?

DID YOU DEACTIVATE THEIR *SELF-EVOLVING* MODES LIKE I TOLD YOU? *NO!* NO, I DON'T THINK YOU *DID!*

BUT SIDNEY, *HE'S* NOT THE ONE TO *WORRY* ABOUT. IT'S HIS SIS--

STOP...?

DO IT, BORIS...
URRRRR...

DO IT!

SKABOOM

YOUR PLACE IS GREAT, SELINA, DON'T GET ME WRONG. HECK, IT'S A LOT BETTER THAN MINE.
BUT, YOU KNOW, MOST OF MY STUFF IS THERE. MY CLOTHES, MY MUSIC...
AND I'M GETTING SICK OF HEARING NOTHING BUT OLD JAZZ.
SO, DID YOU COME UP WITH ANY BRILLIANT IDEAS FOR WIPING MY SLATE CLEAN?...
WHAT ABOUT ASKING, WELL, YOU KNOW...
WHO?
OH. HIM. WELL, HE HAS THE RESOURCES, THAT'S FOR SURE.
BAH BAH BAH.
WOMAN WHO CALLS HERSELF "ORACLE." SHE COVERS ALL HIS HACKING NEEDS.
BAH BAH!
"SHE HAS A COMPUTER LAYOUT LIKE YOU WOULDN'T BELIEVE. SHE COULD SLIP INTO THE POLICE COMPUTERS, SNATCH A FEW LINES OF DATA...
"AND NO ONE...
"I MEAN NO ONE...
"WOULD BE THE WISER."

THEN *WHY* DON'T YOU JUST--

BECAUSE HE *CAN'T* KNOW WHAT HAPPENED. HE CAN'T KNOW THAT I *KILLED* SOMEONE IN COLD BLOOD.

HE HAS HIS *LIMITS,* HOLLY. I HAVE TO DO THIS *WITHOUT* HIS HELP.

BEEP

CATWOMAN. OR SELINA. OR IRENA. OR *WHATEVER* YOU'RE CALLING YOURSELF THESE DAYS.

I WAS *WONDERING* WHEN YOU'D CALL.

BUT UNFORTUNATELY, I'VE GOT SOME *CLIENTS* HERE AT THE MOMENT.
CAN I PUT YOU ON *HOLD?*

WHAT? SURE, I--
GREAT. BE WITH YOU IN A SECOND.
GOTHAM

WHAT'S GOING ON?
I'M NOT SURE.
BAH BAH BAH
YOU GUYS WANT IN, RIGHT?
THAT'S WHY YOU SPENT YOUR LIFE SAVINGS ON THOSE BLACK MARKET GENETIC UPGRADES?
YOU WANT ME TO PUT IN A GOOD WORD WITH MY FORMER COLLEAGUES?
HELL YEAH!
THEN HERE'S THE DEAL.
THERE'S A WOMAN--
A SINGLE, NON-POWERED WOMAN-- ON HER WAY OVER HERE.
STOP HER-- AND YOU'RE IN.
ONE WOMAN.
NO POWERS.
PIECE OF CAKE.
NICE TO SEE CHIVALRY ISN'T DEAD.
KLIK
STILL THERE?
STILL HERE.
LET'S DO THIS IN PERSON. BE OVER HERE IN HALF AN HOUR.
AND WEAR A COSTUME, OKAY?
I HAVE STANDARDS TO UPHOLD.

WHAT A MESS.
HEY, LENAHAN.
LENAHAN.
LENAHAN!
UHHH?
THUD
WHAT THE...?
WORTH? JEEZ, MAN. LISTEN, YOU GOTTA BE CAREFUL WITH THESE FILES.
I PUT WEEKS INTO COMPILING THIS STUFF.
THAT'S EXACTLY WHAT THE LIEUTENANT WANTS TO TALK TO YOU ABOUT.
FIVE MINUTES. HIS OFFICE.
YOU MIGHT WANT TO SHAVE.

BUT WHY CAN'T I GO WITH YOU? THIS IS MY MESS YOU'RE CLEANING UP, RIGHT?
RIGHT. AND THAT'S EXACTLY WHY YOU CAN'T GO. THE WHOLE IDEA IS TO KEEP YOU OUT OF JAIL, REMEMBER?
WAIT. YOU'RE GOING IN COSTUME?
THAT'S WHAT IT'S FOR, HOLLY. TO KEEP MY SECRET IDENTITY SECRET.
BYE BYE, BABY. MOMMY'LL BE HOME SOON.
BUT, DON'T YOU WANT TO--
HOLLY. RELAX.
IT'S GOING TO BE OKAY. I PROMISE.
AFTER ALL...
WHAT COULD POSSIBLY GO WRONG?

WHAT'S THE MATTER, JIM?
YOU USED TO BE ONE OF MY BEST. MY ABSOLUTE BEST. A GO-TO GUY.
SURE, YOU CUT A FEW CORNERS, LEFT A FEW BRUISES, BUT THAT'S ALL IN A DAY'S WORK, ISN'T IT?
SOMETIMES YOU HAVE TO BREAK THE LAW TO UPHOLD THE LAW, RIGHT?
RIGHT.
BUT THIS, WHAT YOU'RE DOING NOW. IT'S DIFFERENT. IT'S A WASTE OF YOUR TIME. AND THAT MAKES IT A WASTE OF MY TIME.
I'VE SEEN IT HAPPEN BEFORE. ESPECIALLY IN GOTHAM...
...YOU SEE PEOPLE IN COSTUMES DO WHAT THEY WANT, AND FIGURE YOU'LL DO THE SAME.
BUT LET ME TELL YOU, JIM. YOU WON'T. NOT ON MY WATCH. LEAVE THE OBSESSIVE BEHAVIOR TO THEM. I NEED YOU CLOSING CASES.
YOU'RE FIXATING ON WHETHER THE LADY IN THE CAT SUIT KILLED THE GUY WITH THE SKULL HEAD. WANT AN ANSWER? HERE'S YOUR ANSWER: NO ONE CARES.
BUT...
BUT NOTHING. YOU'RE IGNORING OTHER CASES, MAKING MISTAKES-- IN PUBLIC, YET-- AND NOW SOME PIZZA GUY IS SUING THE DEPARTMENT.
HIM AND THE MULTINATIONAL COMPANY HE WORKS FOR. NICE, JIM. NICE WORK.
BUT I'M CLOSE, SIR. I'M SO CLOSE.
NO. YOU'RE FAR. YOU'RE VERY FAR. YOU WANT IT STRAIGHT? NOT ENOUGH OF A DETECTIVE TO PUT THESE CLUES TOGETHER? FINE. I'LL GIVE IT TO YOU STRAIGHT.
YOU GET TO WORK ON ANOTHER CASE-- A REAL CASE-- OR YOU CAN TRADE THAT BADGE IN FOR A CAPE AND HANG OUT WITH THE REST OF THE LUNATICS.
UNDERSTAND?
YES, SIR.
I UNDERSTAND PERFECTLY.

Light's on. He really is expecting me.
Too bad. Breaking into his low-budget, high-tech joint would be a nice challenge.
Oh well. Maybe next time.
UNGH!
What the...?
WE ARE TRIPLE THREAT!
THE LATEST CONCEPT IN MODERN CRIMINAL DESIGN!
AND YOU WON'T BE GETTING PAST US!
Calculator.
I'm going to kill that idiot.

SORRY, CATWOMAN, BUT YOU'RE THE ONLY THING STANDING BETWEEN US AND THE TOP RANKS OF TODAY'S LAWBREAKERS.
YOU UNDERSTAND. IT'S NOTHING PERSONAL.

WELL, AS LONG AS WE'RE NOT BEING PERSONAL, I'D LIKE TO OFFER A LITTLE CONSTRUCTIVE CRITICISM ABOUT YOUR COSTUME.
REALLY? HA! LIKE WHAT?
Normally, I wouldn't stoop to this level. Normally, I'd find another way. A more respectable solution. Maybe the whip.

Normally.

LIKE YOU SHOULD'VE PADDED THE CROTCH.

RRR!
YOU'VE GOT A QUICK WIT.

LET'S SEE IF IT'S QUICK ENOUGH TO DODGE THIS.
Nice going, Selina. Focusing more on being cute than being smart. And this guy's a lot stronger than his gravity-defying buddy.
A lot stronger.

THAP
WHAT THE HELL ARE YOU DOING? QUIT SCREWING AROUND AND BLAST HER!
I'M TRYING, DAMMIT!
ZOT
OW!
That tears it.
Normally, I'd take it easy on these morons.
Normally.
SNAP
YAAAAAH!

OHGOD! OHGOD! OHGOD!
THAT'S TWO OF YOU CLOWNS DOWN FOR THE COUNT.
CARE TO GO FOR THREE, STRONG MAN?
WELL?
DIDN'T THINK SO.
KRAK
I'LL TELL OUR HOST YOU WON'T BE JOINING US.

HERE.
I'D HAVE BROUGHT YOU A *COMPLETE SET,* BUT THE GUY IN BLACK IS PROBABLY HALFWAY TO *METROPOLIS* BY NOW.

YOU MIGHT WANT TO CALL AN *AMBULANCE* WHEN YOU GET A CHANCE.
WHITE HAS A BROKEN *ARM,* AND RED...
WELL, LET'S JUST SAY HE COULD PROBABLY USE SOME *MEDICAL* ATTENTION. OR AT LEAST AN *ICE* PACK.

OH, AND YOU OWE ME FORTY BUCKS FOR A NEW *MASK.*
NOW, LET'S GET DOWN TO *BUSINESS.* LET'S TALK ABOUT WHY I FOUGHT THREE GOOFBALLS JUST TO MEET WITH YOU ON SUCH A *SNOWY* NIGHT.

WAIT. LET ME *GUESS.*
YOU WANT ME TO GO INTO THE RECORDS OF THE GOTHAM *POLICE* DEPARTMENT AND ERASE EVERY REFERENCE TO YOUR FRIEND AND SUBSTITUTE CATWOMAN *HOLLY ROBINSON.*

WOW. YOU'RE *GOOD.*
IT'S *INFORMATION,* PURE AND SIMPLE. THAT'S WHAT I DEAL IN. THAT'S *WHY* YOU CALLED ME.

AND NOW THAT WE KNOW WHAT *YOU* WANT...
LET'S TALK ABOUT WHAT *I* WANT.

NOW LET ME GUESS. MONEY, AND LOTS OF IT.
HARDLY. WITH A FEW KEYSTROKES, I CAN TRANSFER MORE FUNDS THAN YOU COULD STEAL IN A LIFETIME. IN NINE LIFETIMES.
WELL THEN I HOPE YOU'RE NOT THINKING OF--
DON'T FLATTER YOURSELF. MY NEEDS ARE SIMPLE AND PURE. ALL I WANT IS A TRINKET. A MEMENTO. A SOUVENIR. LITERALLY.
HERE, LET ME FIND A PICTURE...
THAT? THAT'S WHAT YOU WANT ME TO STEAL?
MM-HMM.
BUT IT'S JUST SOME SNOWGLOBE. THERE MUST BE MILLIONS JUST LIKE IT.
METROPOLIS
I'M SURE THERE ARE. BUT I WANT THIS ONE.
IT'S SPECIAL.
LET ME PULL BACK A BIT. GIVE YOU THE FULL PICTURE.

SEE? IT'S NOT JUST ANY SNOWGLOBE. IT USED TO BELONG TO MY BOSS.
MAYBE YOU RECOGNIZE HIM?
Lex Luthor...
Swell.

TODAY.
OW!
THUMP
And...
HEH.
...it's just that simple.
I'm joking, of course.
I mean, it's never that simple.
EXCUSE ME.

YESTERDAY.
Turner Classics was showing "Cat People" for the millionth time last week, and it got me thinking about something Holly asked me.
About why, with all the names in the world, why I picked the alias I did.
Why I named myself after Irena Dubrovna, the movie's lead character.
Well, obviously, the whole "Cat People" angle was part of it...
But that wasn't the only reason. I have a little more depth than that.
I feel a connection to Irena. Always have.
There's a great moment in "Cat People" where she describes how she prefers night to day.
"I like the dark," she says. "It is friendly."
She's right. It is friendly. I suppose that's why I love Gotham so much.
It's dark. It's cozy.
It's home.
This place, on the other hand...
187
CITIZEN LEX

It's just too damned sunny.
MMVI
Welcome to
METROPOLIS

Lunch wasn't bad. A tad too saucy, but pretty decent overall. Better than I would've thought, anyway.

Maybe this quaint little town isn't so awful after all.

What are they all...?

LOOK!

Oh.

Right.

As much as I'd like to stand around and gawk at the local tourist attractions...
...I have to get going.
This is a business trip, after all.

A WEEK AGO.
BUT IT'S JUST SOME SNOWGLOBE. THERE MUST BE MILLIONS JUST LIKE IT.
I'M SURE THERE ARE. BUT I WANT THIS ONE.
IT'S SPECIAL.
METROPOLIS
IT USED TO BELONG TO MY OLD BOSS.
Lex Luthor. Ex-President, ex-billionaire, not-yet-ex-evil genius. Yeah, I recognize him.
Why can't these things ever be easy?
Of course, if it were easy, Calculator could get anyone to do it.
I'm the only one with a shot. Just like he's the only one who can perform my little homework assignment.
Wipe Holly's name out of the G.C.P.D. computers.
So they never arrest her for the murder.
MAYBE YOU RECOGNIZE HIM?
The one I committed.

I've done my research. quasi-legal web sites, bootleg blueprints, you name it.
I've studied this building for days. Cased it from every angle. All except for one. This one.
Inside.
...BECAUSE LEXCORP IS PROUDEST OF ITS EFFORTS TO MAKE THE WORLD A BETTER PLACE. BRAINS MAY HAVE BUILT LEXCORP...
BUT ITS DRIVING FORCE REMAINS ITS HEART.
NOW, BEFORE WE PROCEED TO THE ROOFTOP LOUNGE FOR COMPLIMENTARY SNACKS, ARE THERE ANY QUESTIONS?
Yes, its jet-black heart. Other C.E.O.s get tossed out after charges of insider trading, securities fraud, that sort of thing.
But LexCorp's ex-chief? Mass-murder.
YES? THE LADY IN THE GOTHAM KNIGHTS CAP?
IS THERE SOMETHING YOU'D LIKE TO KNOW ABOUT LEXCORP?
MAYBE ABOUT LANA LANG, THE NEW C.E.O. WHO'S GOING TO GUIDE US INTO A GLORIOUS NEW ERA?
NOT EXACTLY. I HAVE A QUESTION ABOUT YOUR OLD C.E.O.
YOU KNOW, THE BALD GUY?
LIKE, WHERE'S ALL HIS STUFF?

WELL?
ERR...YES, SOME OF OUR GUESTS ARE INTERESTED IN THE MORE... CONTROVERSIAL ASPECTS OF LEXCORP HISTORY.
BUT LET ME ASSURE YOU, WE'VE MOVED PAST THE DAYS OF LEX LUTHOR AND ENSURED THEY WON'T RETURN TO TROUBLE US-- OR THE REST OF THE WORLD.
LEX LUTHOR'S TERRIBLE LEGACY, IN FACT, LIES BURIED FAR BENEATH OUR FEET.
DON'T WORRY. THE EXPERIMENTS, INVENTIONS AND POSSESSIONS YOU'VE HEARD RUMORS ABOUT ARE SAFELY PUT AWAY, BENEATH TONS OF STEEL AND CONCRETE.
IN FACT, THERE'S ONLY ONE MAN IN THE WORLD WHO CAN GET INTO THE VAULT...
IF YOU'RE LUCKY, MAYBE YOU'LL CATCH A GLIMPSE OF HIM IN THE ROOFTOP ATRIUM.
JUST BE SURE TO LOOK... UP IN THE SKY.

NOW, IF YOU'LL *JUST* FOLLOW ME...
NO ADMITTANCE
And that's my cue.
Have to do this before the crowd gets too far away...
or it's going to look too...
Bingo.
PLIK
NO ADMITTANCE
Nice to know that motherhood hasn't dulled the old job skills.

Figures. Camera in a maintenance tunnel.
Guess LexCorp is worried someone's going to steal these pipes.

Maybe they're made out of some space-age magic metal. Maybe they are incalculably valuable.
Or maybe Lex Luthor's company has inherited his paranoia. For their sake, I hope they have...

Because I'm here to rob them blind.

Well, sort of.
Holly, this had better be one hell of a snow globe.

GOTHAM CITY.
NO! HOLLY, YOU ARE NOT DOING THIS!
THE HELL I'M NOT.
THAT LITTLE GIRL IS GOING TO DIE IF SOMEONE DOESN'T FIND HER SOON, AND WITH SELINA IN METROPOLIS, I'M THE ONLY ONE WHO HAS A CHANCE.
YOU THINK THOSE COPS ARE GOING TO FIND HER? IN THE EAST END? PLEASE.
AMBER ALERT
BREAKING NEWS
BUT SELINA'S TRYING TO KEEP YOU OUT OF JAIL. YOU SHOW YOUR FACE IN PUBLIC, ESPECIALLY IN THAT COSTUME...
YOU'RE GOING RIGHT BACK. THIS TIME FOR GOOD.
I HAVE TO WEAR THE COSTUME, KARON. IT'S MADE FOR THIS SORT OF THING. LEATHER, HEAVY BOOTS, CLAWS IN THE GLOVES...
PLUS, THERE'S A CERTAIN PSYCHOLOGICAL BONUS. BELIEVE ME.
HOLLY, SELINA WILL BE BACK SOON. WHY CAN'T YOU JUST WAIT?
WHAT IF IT WAS HELENA?
WOULD YOU STILL WANT ME TO WAIT?
I DIDN'T THINK SO.
NOW DO ME A FAVOR AND OPEN THE WINDOW.

Police radio on the helmet headset.
Don't know where she got it-- or stole it-- but it works like a charm.
Cops. Stupid cops.
They'll never find that kid. Not until it's way too late.
But me, I've got lots of friends in the East End.
Well-informed friends.
'Course, the East End is miles from here. No way I'd make it on foot.
Not in time to stop somebody from dying.
GCPD
But like I said, that police radio works like a charm.
Ha.
If Selina could see me now.

SUB BASEMENT 12
NO ADMITTANCE
THIP
WHA?
WHAP
UNGH!
OOOH...
NO YOU DON'T.
NO ADMITTANCE
One guard? In a corporation that employs, what? millions?
And a lock that, frankly, is beneath my abilities.
That's it?
Then again, maybe that's all you need...

When you're protecting nothing.
No doors, no windows, no hatches, vents or pipes.
HMMM.
No crawlspaces, cracks, ducts, soft spots or weak spots.
A dozen feet of concrete-- at least-- then three more of steel...
Then more concrete.
Then more steel.
Our perky little tour guide was right. There's no way into that vault.
Unless, of course, you cheat.
Here's where I play with my new toy...

YESTERDAY
His name's Warp. A.K.A. Emil Lasalle.
Supervillain. Teleporter.
Sound sleeper.
Bad for him.
Good for me.

Calculator tipped me off that a) he was in Gotham, and b) he was working on some sort of teleporting device.
Warp doesn't need it, obviously. He can do that without any help. He was going to sell this gizmo. Or trade it. Or auction it off.

Doesn't matter. It's mine now.
Sometimes, it takes a little theft to make a bigger one possible.

Now...
...Assuming I made all the proper connections, hooked up the right batteries and typed in the right coordinates...
...everything's going to be fine.
HERE GOES NOTHING.
TCHIK
FSSH
PAF

SOMEWHERE OVER SOUTHEASTERN ALASKA...

<WELL, BORIS?>

<NO PURSUIT, NATASHA. *NONE* AT ALL.>

<OF COURSE NOT. THAT PRISONER TRANSFER WAS *COVERT*, A BOTCHED PLAN BETWEEN TWO BUREAUCRATS MEANT TO *FURTHER* THEIR CAREERS.>

<EVERYONE WHO KNEW ABOUT IT IS *DEAD*.>

<EVERYONE BUT *US*.>

<AND *NOW* WHAT? BACK HOME? BACK TO MOTHER *RUSSIA*?>
<HARDLY. THEY'D *HANG* US FOR WHAT WE'VE DONE. THE RUSSIA WE GREW UP IN IS GONE, BORIS. *RED* SQUARE IS FULL OF *GOLDEN* ARCHES.>

<NO, I HAVE *ANOTHER* IDEA. THAT WOMAN WHO PUT US IN PRISON. THE CAT. REMEMBER *HER*? I'D LIKE TO PAY HER A VISIT.>
<NOW WHERE DID SHE LIVE AGAIN? AH, YES.>

<GOTHAM.>
<THE *EAST* END.>
<HOW FITTING.>
GOTHAM CITY
East End

OOP...
FEEL LIKE...
LIKE...
LIKE...
WOW.

THIS...
I MEAN...
Seems like a waste to go to so much trouble to get in here...
And then just steal a snow globe.

I mean, like the man said, I'm a world-class thief, right? I might as well take advantage of the situation.
After all, it's not like anyone's going to miss...

Wait. Someone's coming.

But how...?

...And who?

WHAT THE HELL?
WHAT THE HELL?

YOU? ME? BUT...
WAIT. I REMEMBER THIS. LISTEN...
YOU NEED TO WATCH OUT FOR THE LOO...

WHAT WAS THAT?!?

Calm down, Selina. Could've been anything. Illusion generator. Parallel dimension portal. Hypnosis device.
Luthor was into some pretty crazy stuff.

What I need to do is quit screwing around and focus on the job at hand.

There's no telling what else is lurking in a place like this...

BLIP

HUMMMMMMM

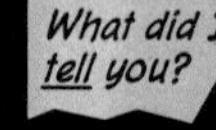
What did I tell you?

Now see, this...
This is the sort of thing I should have expected.
It fits in with Luthor's whole Metropolis mad scientist motif.
I mean, back in Gotham, who's going to go to the trouble to...
WH-CHUNK
YOWZA!
All that money... all that ice...
And thanks to Robby the Robot here, I can't even snag any.
These boxes... there's gotta be something that'll stop that ...
KRUNK
NGH!

Ow. That's a rib.
THOOM
URK!
Just need a...
BINGO.
SMILE, TIN MAN.
KRAKOOOOOOM

BOOOM

THUMP
OW!
Well, that should solve my killer robot problem.
Now if I can only...

And...
HEH.
...it's just that simple.

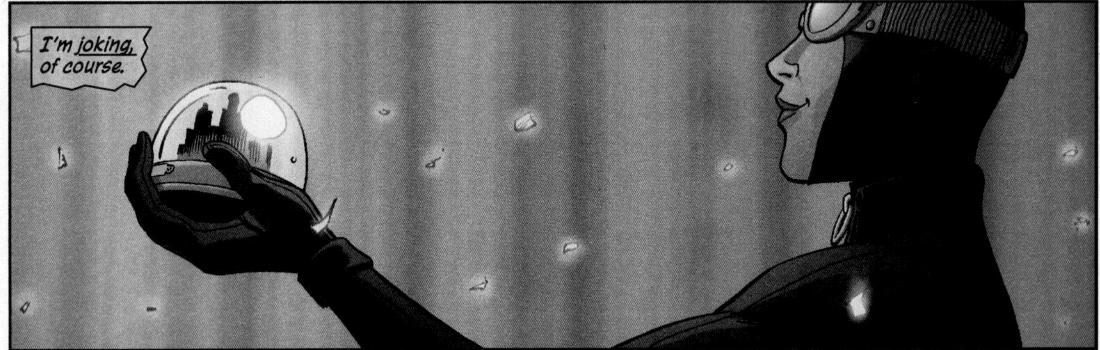
I'm joking, of course.

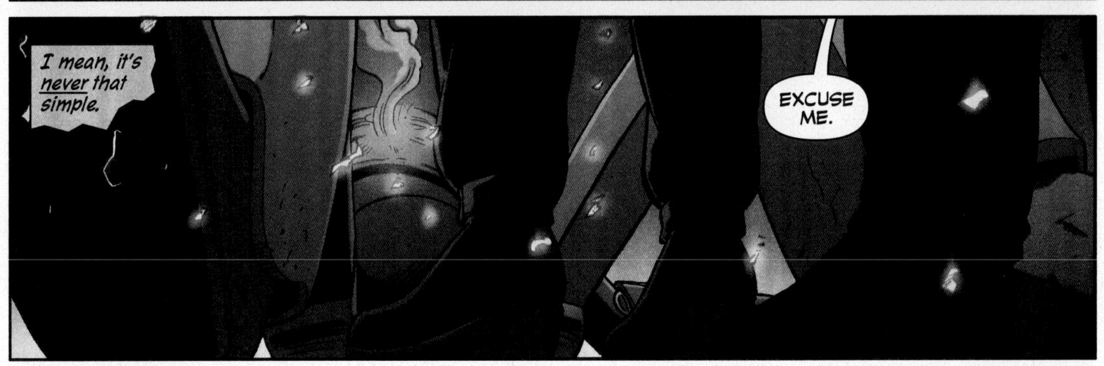
I mean, it's never that simple.
EXCUSE ME.

BUT I BELIEVE THAT BELONGS TO *ME.*
See?
What did I tell you?

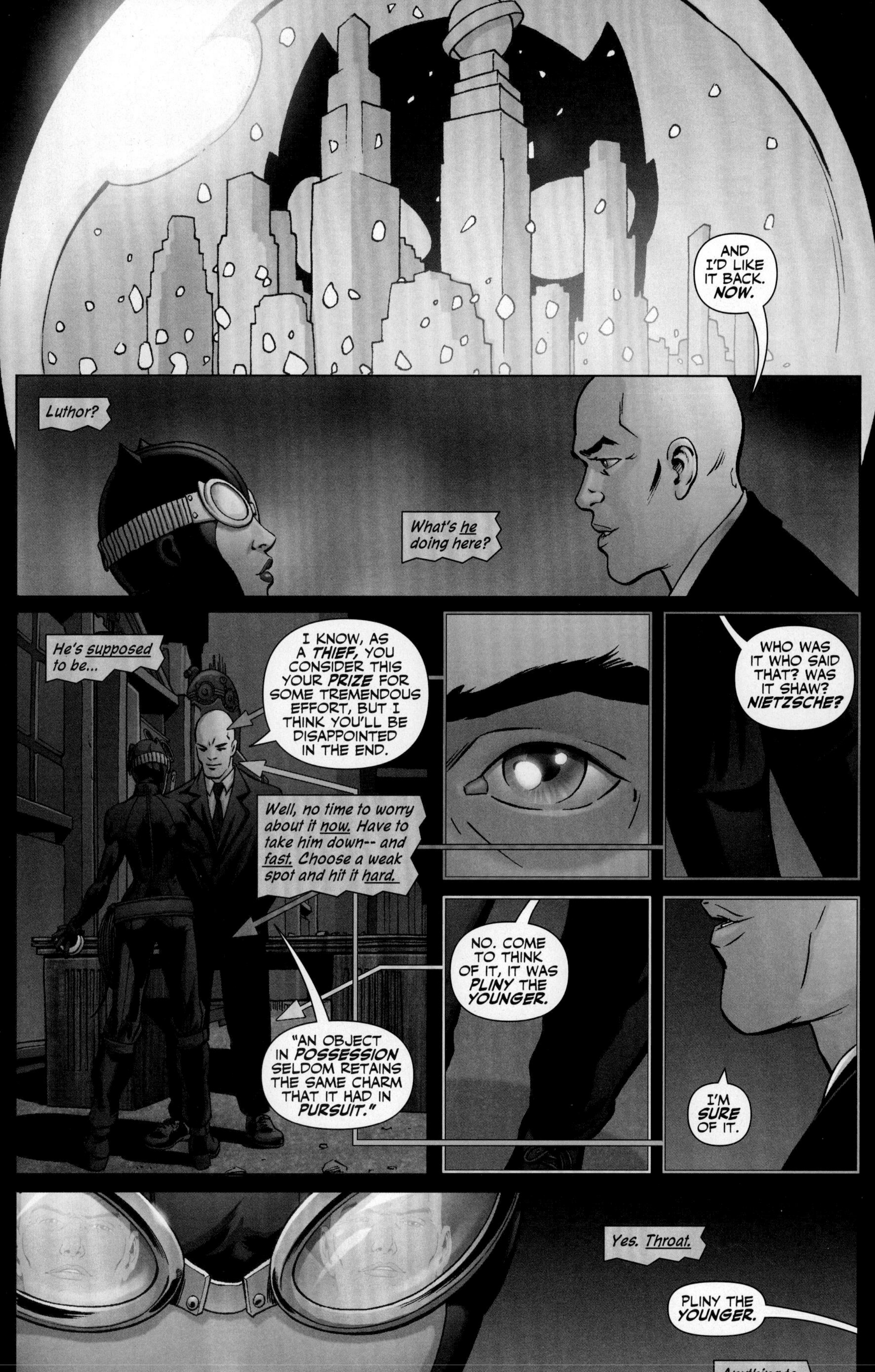
AND I'D LIKE IT BACK. NOW.
Luthor?
What's he doing here?
He's supposed to be...
I KNOW, AS A THIEF, YOU CONSIDER THIS YOUR PRIZE FOR SOME TREMENDOUS EFFORT, BUT I THINK YOU'LL BE DISAPPOINTED IN THE END.
Well, no time to worry about it now. Have to take him down-- and fast. Choose a weak spot and hit it hard.
"AN OBJECT IN POSSESSION SELDOM RETAINS THE SAME CHARM THAT IT HAD IN PURSUIT."
WHO WAS IT WHO SAID THAT? WAS IT SHAW? NIETZSCHE?
NO. COME TO THINK OF IT, IT WAS PLINY THE YOUNGER.
I'M SURE OF IT.
Yes. Throat.
PLINY THE YOUNGER.
Anything to shut him up.

What the...?

NOT CONVINCED?

Since when is he so...

Fast?

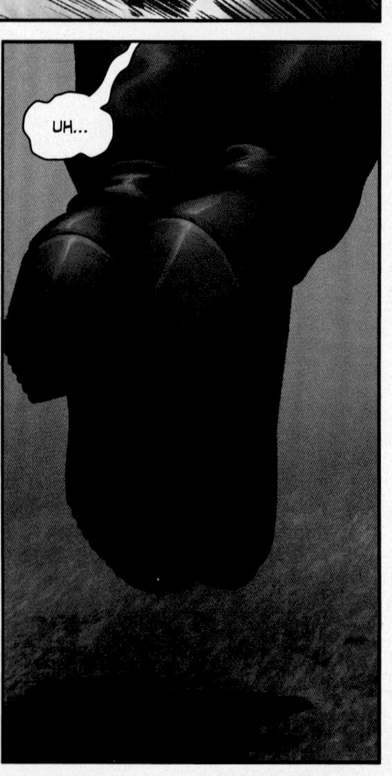

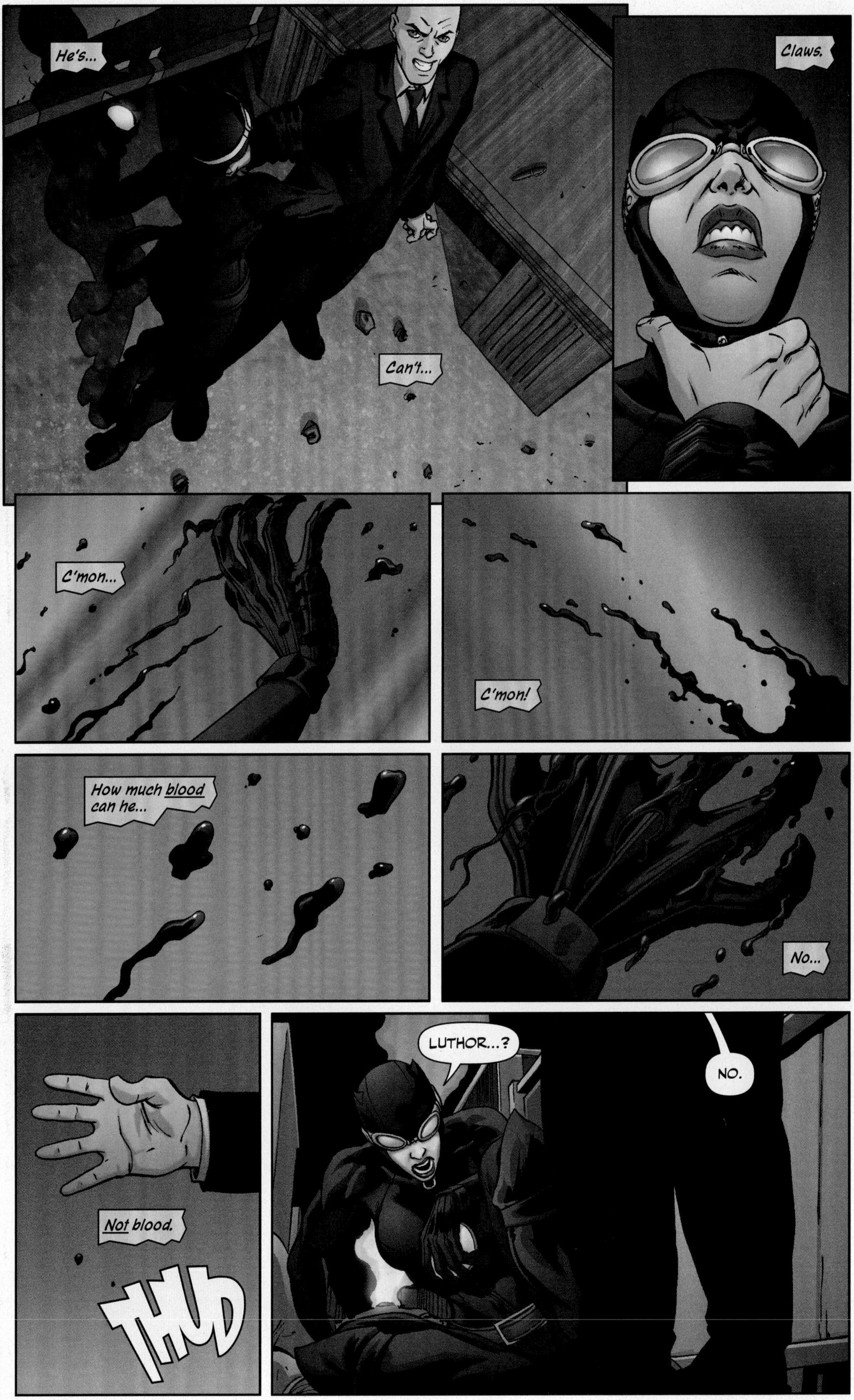

He's...

Claws.

Can't...

C'mon...

C'mon!

How much *blood* can he...

No...

BUT *CLOSE.*
VERY, *VERY* CLOSE.

A robot. A killer Lex Luthor robot.
That figures.

Not being a fool, I run.
Fast.

It's not even the robot that worries me. Not exactly.
HMM.
Here's what worries me:

He's not in any sort of a hurry.

WELL, NOW.
THAT'S JUST A DAMNED SHAME.
He's acting like he's got all the time in the world.

IT'S NEVER EASY TO SEE ONE OF YOUR ANCESTORS COME TO A BAD END.
IT WAS CRUDE DEVICES LIKE HIM THAT MADE ME POSSIBLE, YOU SEE.
Think, Selina. Think!
There has to be something among all these doo-dads and widgets that can stop that thing.
THOUGH I'M OBVIOUSLY SEVERAL MILLION UPGRADES AWAY FROM THAT WORLD'S FAIR CURIOSITY. THE PERFECT SIMULATION OF HUMANITY-- VASTLY IMPROVED.
Glad to see LexCorp remembered to install the ego chip.
Just wouldn't be the same without it.
Say... this looks promising.
WHAT'S THAT? FOUND YOURSELF A TOY?
URK... URK...
PLAY WITH THIS, YOU SON OF A--
WOOOOM

THAT'S DONE.

Time to fire up Warp's rig and get back upstairs.

Oh, no. It Figures. Warp's gadget doesn't even work?
CLICK
CLICK
CLICK

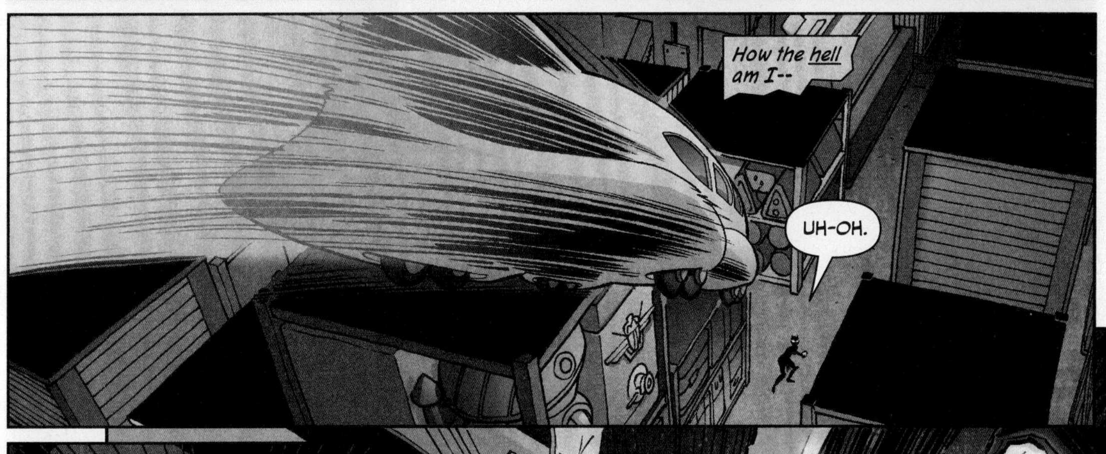
How the hell am I--
UH-OH.

UHHH?
NOW THEN.
WHY DON'T YOU STAND UP SO WE CAN DISCUSS MATTERS FACE TO FACE.
OF COURSE, THAT DOES PUT ME AT A DISADVANTAGE, BEING THAT MUCH OF MY FACE IS NO LONGER ATTACHED TO MY HEAD.
AND SO, BEING THE GENTLEMAN THAT I AM...
WIRRRRRRRR
IT THINK IT'S HIGH TIME I RETURNED THE FAVOR.

Figures. Even a Lex Luthor robot is murderously self-centered.
WIRRRRRRR
URK!

Need a second to think. Gotta get away. Somewhere... any--

HUH?

WHAT THE HELL?
WHAT THE HELL?

YOU? ME? BUT...
OH. I REMEMBER THIS. LISTEN...
YOU NEED TO WATCH OUT FOR THE LOO--

--THOR ROBOT.
DAMN.

DAMN INDEED.

YOU'RE BACK. I KNEW YOU WOULD BE.
THAT DEVICE SENDS YOU FOUR MINUTES INTO THE PAST AND A TWO DOZEN YARDS TO THE EAST. UNFORTUNATELY, THE EFFECT ONLY LASTS TWELVE SECONDS.
TRAVELERS BOUNCE BACK TO WHERE-- AND WHEN-- THEY STARTED. TRAGIC, REALLY. THE DEVICE WAS MEANT TO DO SO MUCH MORE.
WE-- AND BY THAT, I MEAN HE-- COULD NEVER GET IT TO WORK PROPERLY. ONE OF HIS FEW FAILURES. THAT'S WHY IT'S DOWN HERE, COLLECTING DUST.
THAT'S WHY YOU DON'T LIVE IN A WORLD THAT WORSHIPS LEX LUTHOR AS A GOD. THAT HAS ALWAYS WORSHIPPED LEX LUTHOR AS A GOD.
SAD, ISN'T IT?
BUT ENOUGH WISTFUL THINKING. ENOUGH TALK ABOUT WHAT MIGHT HAVE BEEN.
IT'S TIME TO FACE REALITY.
IT'S TIME TO KILL YOU.

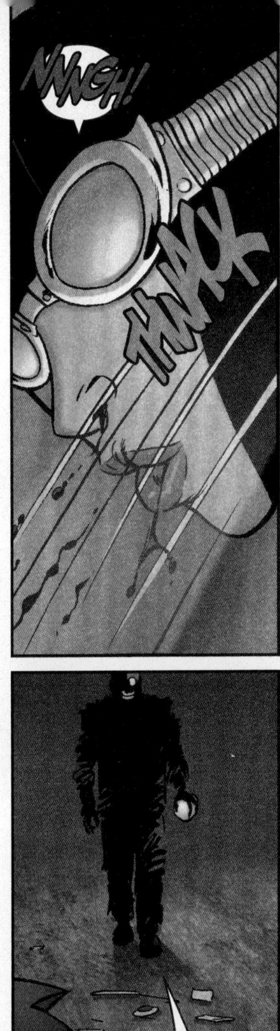
NNGH!
THWACK

Concentrate, damn it! Focus! You have to stay...
UHHH...

Wait... what's he doing?
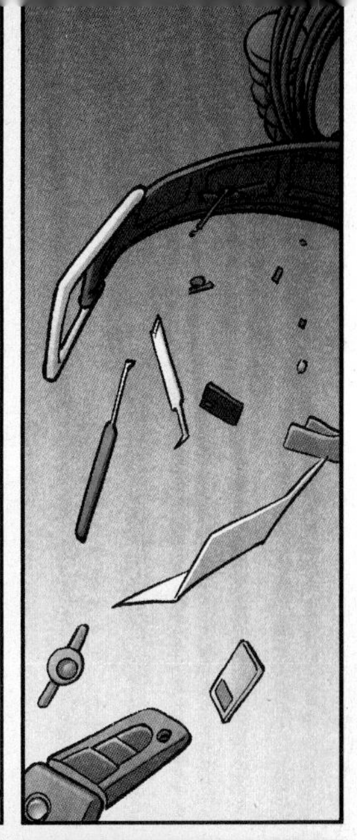

STILL CONSCIOUS? STILL ALIVE?
I'M IMPRESSED.

HMM.
WHAT'S SO IMPORTANT YOU'D CARRY IT INTO BATTLE?
MUST BE SOMEONE VERY NEAR AND DEAR TO YOUR HEART.

What the...?

What is that?

AH, YES.
SUCH A BEAUTIFUL CHILD.
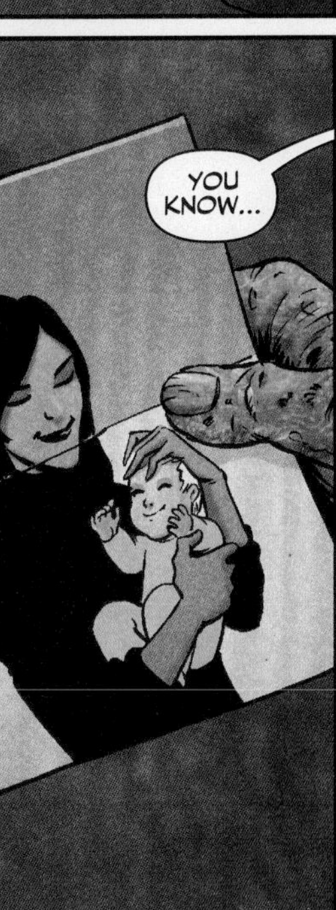
YOU KNOW...

I THINK I'D LIKE TO MEET HER.
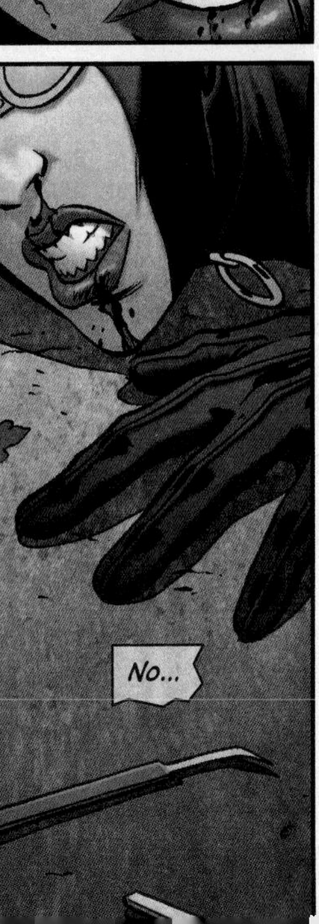
No...

NO...
NOOOOOO!
EH?
ONE LAST DESPERATE MOVE TO SAVE YOUR DAUGHTER. HOW TOUCHING.
I'LL DO YOU A FAVOR AND END THIS QUICKLY.
I HAVE SEVERAL THOUSAND VOLTS OF ELECTRICITY COURSING THROUGH MY VEINS.
AND NOW...
SO DO YOU.

ZZZZZZZT
N-NICE TRY, BALDY MCBALD, BUT IT'S GOING TO TAKE MORE THAN THAT. A LOT MORE.
Lucky thing this suit is insanely insulated.
Lucky. Lucky. Lucky.
PLEASE. HAVE SOME DIGNITY. LET'S STOP PROLONGING THIS. AFTER ALL, WE BOTH KNOW HOW IT'S GOING TO END. IT'S INEVITABLE.
"I MUST BE CRUEL ONLY TO BE KIND." DO YOU KNOW WHAT GREAT MAN SAID THAT?
NICK LOWE?
AMUSING TO THE BITTER END, EH? NO. SHAKESPEARE.
SORRY.
BUT, IF IT'S ANY CONSOLATION, YOU ARE MOVING ON TO FINAL JEOPARDY.
YOU'LL PARDON, OF COURSE, THE POP CULTURE REFERENCE.
"AN ENEMY'S DEATH SHOULD BE SAVORED LIKE A FINE WINE, A GOOD CIGAR, OR A HEARTY MEAL."
DO YOU KNOW WHO SAID THAT?
PLINY THE YOUNGER?
HA. NO, SORRY AGAIN. WRONG ANSWER.

IT WAS ME.
JUST BEFORE I KILLED YOU.
Ego chip...

I love you.
THUK

ZZZT

ZZZT

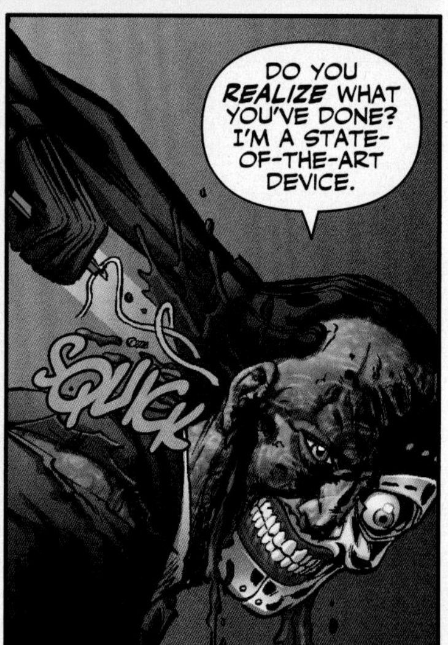
DO YOU REALIZE WHAT YOU'VE DONE? I'M A STATE-OF-THE-ART DEVICE.
SQUICK

I'M WORTH BILLIONS. I'M DESIGNED NOT TO FALL INTO THE WRONG HANDS.
PRECAUTIONS HAVE BEEN TAKEN. IF I PERISH, SO DOES ANYONE EVEN REMOTELY NEAR ME.

DON'T BOTHER TO RUN. THE BLAST WON'T DESTROY EVERYTHING IN THIS ROOM, BUT IT WILL--
ZZZT
--CERTAINLY DESTROY YOU.
ZZZT
EITHER THE SHOCK WAVE OR THE FLASH OF HEAT. ONE OF THEM WILL KILL YOU. MOST PROBABLY--
ZZZT
BOTH. AT ANY RATE, THERE'S NOWHERE TO HIDE.

YOINK!
THE PAPER-WEIGHT? HA! TAKE IT! IT'LL BE SHATTERED TO DUST NO MATTER WHAT CORNER YOU DUCK INTO.

WHERE ARE YOU--
ZZZT
--GOING? THERE'S NOWHERE YOU CAN HIDE! NOWHERE THAT WILL SAVE YOU!

REALLY?
NOT EVEN FOUR MINUTES AGO?

KZZZNATTT

SEE YOU IN THE FUNNY PAPERS.

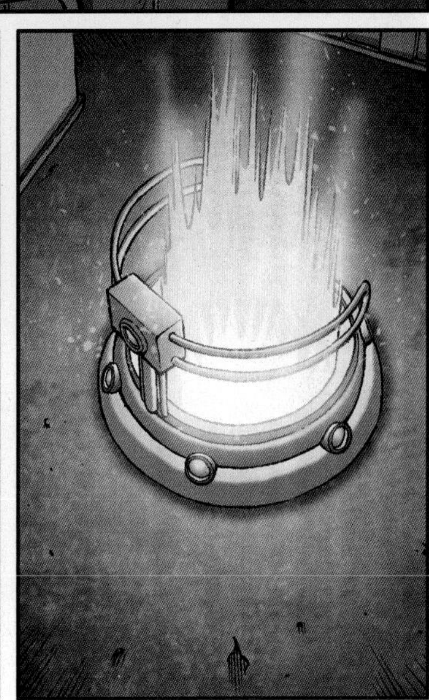

HMM.
SHE REALLY IS A CLEVER GIRL.
BOOOM
HA.
IT WORKED.
IT'S TIME TO FACE REALITY.
IT'S TIME TO KILL YOU.
Now that... that's creepy.

WOW.
At least I don't have to worry about finding a way out of here.
Just go up...
And up...
And out.
UHHH...
WHO... HEY!
HEY YOURSELF.
THOKK
NOW, SEXY...
LET'S SEE ABOUT GETTING YOU OUT OF THAT UNIFORM.

In all the post-blast hubbub, no one notices one more Lexcorp security stooge.
Even if she is a lot smaller, and walking in the opposite direction.
No cops. No fire and rescue. No ambulances.
Guess LexCorp handles their messes internally.
Must figure one of their gizmos downstairs blew up all by itself.
Well, they're half right. It doesn't matter.
What matters is I'm out, I'm in one piece...
And I got what I came for.
DENNISON
Hallelujah.
EXCUSE ME.
No.
Not now.

BUT I DON'T THINK THAT BELONGS TO YOU.
Figures.

Hell...
I'm surprised I didn't run into him sooner.

WELL?

LISTEN. I'M HURT, I'M TIRED, AND I NEED TO MAKE A PHONE CALL. HONESTLY, ALL I DID WAS STEAL A FIVE-DOLLAR SNOW GLOBE.

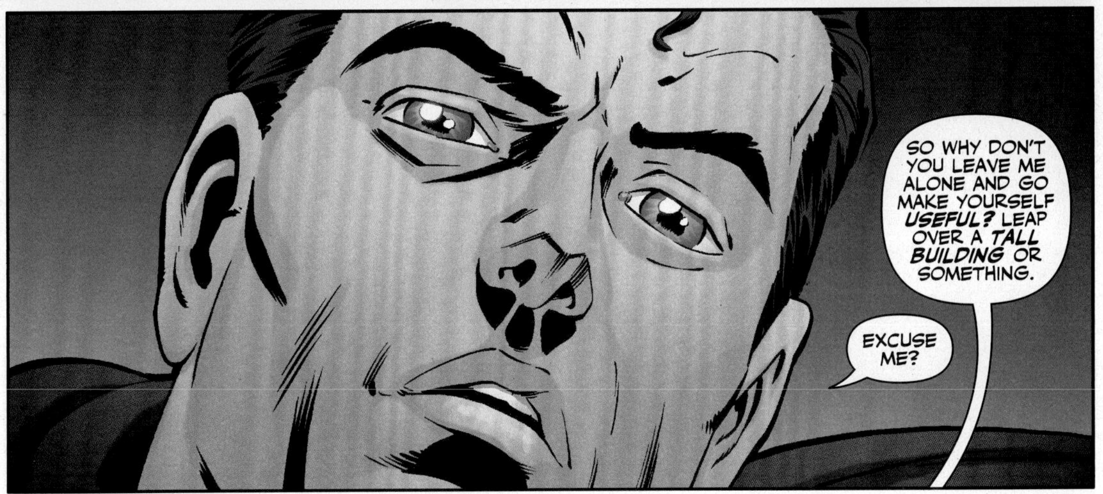
SO WHY DON'T YOU LEAVE ME ALONE AND GO MAKE YOURSELF USEFUL? LEAP OVER A TALL BUILDING OR SOMETHING.
EXCUSE ME?

IT'S A SNOW GLOBE. REALLY. THAT'S ALL. GIVE IT THE OLD X-RAY ONCE OVER. KNOW WHAT YOU'LL SEE?
YOU'LL SEE SNOW-- OR WHATEVER THOSE LITTLE WHITE FLAKES ARE MADE OF.
IT'S JUST A CHEAP SOUVENIR, BUT IT CAN HELP SOMEONE. IT CAN HELP THEM A LOT. THAT'S WHY I WENT TO SO MUCH TROUBLE TO STEAL IT.

YOU'RE SUPERMAN.
YOU TELL ME IF I'M LYING.

I WANT YOU OUT OF MY CITY. NOW.
BROTHER, I'M GONE.

"I want you out of my city."
YEESH.
I bet he got that from Bruce.

GOTHAM.
LATER.
YES?
I GOT IT.

I KNEW YOU WOULD.
WAIT A MINUTE. I DON'T RECOGNIZE THIS NUMBER. WHOSE PHONE ARE YOU CALLING ON?

I'M NOT SURE. I SNAGGED IT IN A CROWD.
MINE GOT LOST WHILE I WAS...
IT'S A LONG STORY.

SKIP IT. YOU CAN TELL ME ALL ABOUT IT WHEN YOU GET BACK TO GOTHAM. WE'LL HAVE A FEW DRINKS, I'LL PUT MY SOUVENIR ON THE SHELF...
AND...
AND I'LL WIPE HOLLY'S NAME OUT OF THE POLICE RECORD.

GOOD. I WANT TO GET THAT MESS FIXED AS SOON AS POSSIBLE.
YES. I'LL BET YOU DO.
NOW THAT'S INTERESTING...

SPEAKING OF THAT, THERE'S **SOMETHING** I SHOULD TELL YOU...
WHAT?
EXCUSE ME.
BUT YOU *TOOK* SOMETHING THAT *BELONGS* TO ME.
LISTEN, I'M GOING TO HAVE TO CALL YOU *BACK.*
YEAH.
SOME-THING JUST CAME UP.
MOST DEFINITELY *NOT* THE END...

CAT
IT'S ONLY A MOVIE
WOMAN
COVERS BY ADAM HUGHES

LIQUOR
DRUG STORE

FINE ITAL

AH!

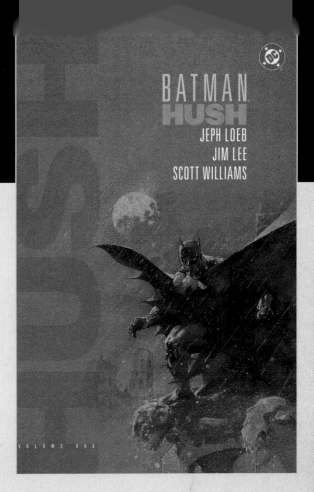